I0421490

Enneagram

The Ultimate Guide to SELF-DISCOVERY through the 9 PERSONALITY TYPES and 27 SUBTYPES – For Beginners Who Wish to Develop their Understanding of Relationships, Leadership, Psychology

© **Copyright 2019 - All rights reserved.**
The content contained within this book may not be reproduced, duplicated or transmitted without direct written permission from the author or the publisher.

Under no circumstances will any blame or legal responsibility be held against the publisher, or author, for any damages, reparation, or monetary loss due to the information contained within this book, either directly or indirectly.

Legal Notice:
This book is copyright protected. It is only for personal use. You cannot amend, distribute, sell, use, quote or paraphrase any part, or the content within this book, without the consent of the author or publisher.

Disclaimer Notice:
Please note the information contained within this document is for educational and entertainment purposes only. All effort has been executed to present accurate, up to date, reliable, complete information. No warranties of any kind are declared or implied. Readers acknowledge that the author is not engaging in the rendering of legal, financial, medical or professional advice. The content within this book has been derived from various sources. Please consult a licensed professional before attempting any techniques outlined in this book.

By reading this document, the reader agrees that under no circumstances is the author responsible for any losses, direct or indirect, that are incurred as a result of the use of information contained within this document, including, but not limited to, errors, omissions, or inaccuracies.

Table of Content

Introduction

In this book you will find detailed descriptions about nine types of personalities. These personalities are what make up the Enneagram theory. Through these personalities, you will not only be able to understand yourself better, but your friends, partners, family, and co-workers.

This book can help start your journey to self-discovery. You will be able to learn your strengths, weaknesses, and how you can turn your weaknesses into strengths. You will learn about the highs of your personality and its lows. All this information will help to transform you into the best person you can become.

This book starts out by explaining what the Enneagram theory is. You will see a few of its diagrams, such as the Enneagram itself and its center points. You will get a brief introduction of the nine personality types and the 27 subtypes, as each personality type consists of three subtypes. You will also learn the benefits of the Enneagram theory.

Starting in chapter 2, you will begin to learn about the types of individual personalities. We will start with the first type of personality, which is the perfectionist. In chapter 3, you will learn about the helper. We will then look into the achiever in chapter 4. Chapter 5 will look at the individualist, which is the fourth personality type. The fifth personality type will be discussed in chapter 6, which is = the investigator. I will talk about the loyalist, in other words the sixth personality type, in chapter 7. The seventh personality type, which is the enthusiast, will be discussed in chapter 8. Chapter 9 will inform you about the protector. And finally, chapter 10 will focus on the ninth personality type, which is the mediator or peacemaker.

Chapter 11 is a special chapter as it focuses on the Enneagram test, which you can take for free online. However, you can always take the time to spend money taking the test elsewhere. This chapter will describe the test, give you a summary of the types, subtypes, and outline the difference between the Enneagram and the Myer-Briggs test.

By the end of this book, you should be able to understand the basics of the Enneagram theory. You should not only know which personality type you have but also be able to identify your strengths, weaknesses, and how you work with other personalities. From this book, you will also be able to identify if you sit at a healthy, average, or unhealthy level of integration. Once you identify your level, you will be able to find ways to help you reach the healthiest level so that you can become the best person you can be.

The Enneagram is more than a test that allows you to learn

what numbered personally you have. It is a test that can give you the information you need in order to make sure you feel your life is being fulfilled to its fullest. At this point, I feel it is important to make sure you realize that everyone makes mistakes and no one is perfect. There are a couple of personalities in the Enneagram that struggle with imperfections. If you fall within one of these personalities, the first step you need to take is to realize that it is okay to be wrong, to struggle, and to not always be happy. However, it is also important to remember your mindset. No matter what personality you have, you will need to keep the right frame of mind if you want to remain at a healthy level with your personality.

Chapter 1: The Theory of Enneagram

No one is 100% certain where the Enneagram theory started. Some people believe it can be traced back mathematically, while others state it started through spirituality and Christianity. Plotinus, a Greek philosopher who lived in 200 A.D, spoke of nine principles of the human personality. Ramon Llull, a mathematician from the 13th century also spoke on nine personality types (Cloete, n.d.).

However, no matter how far back you trace the Enneagram theory, you will find an evolution devoted to it. Today, the Enneagram theory is a diagram which looks to identify a person's personality. However, many psychologists have also used this theory to identify people in large groups (Cloete, n.d.).

How it Works

One of the distinctive factors about the Enneagram theory is it doesn't put people into a box. Within the nine main types of personalities are 27 subtypes. On top of this, in each personality there are wings, lines, and other factors that help determine your unique personality (Cloete, n.d.). While the theory and diagram might seem complicated at first, as it is complex, it becomes easier to understand it the more you learn the details about the types, subtypes, and how the theory works in general.

Diagrams

The Enneagram Diagram

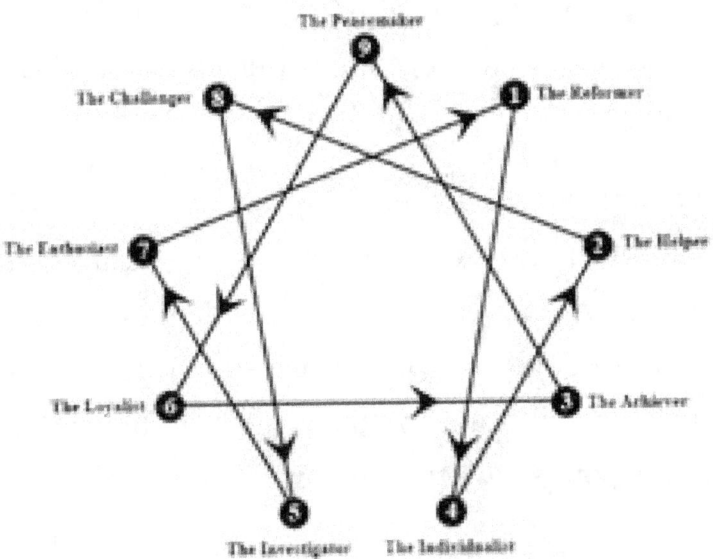

In order to help you understand the diagram of the Enneagram, you will want to look at it step by step. This will help you better understand and follow the basic structure of the Enneagram. For instance, you can start by looking at the diagram as a circle. Around this circle, you will see the numbers nine through one. While the numbers are numerical, if you go counter-clockwise, they are also placed in a systematic order, which is why nine is at the top. Each of these nine numbers represents a personality type, which you can identify in the diagram above.

People often get confused about the lines within the circle. As you can see, there are a variety of lines which go from one number to the next. These are the lines that guide you to your personality and your personality's wings. Again, if you take the lines one by one, you will gain a better understanding of the Enneagram.

First, take a look at numbers nine, six, and three. You will notice that when they are connected, they create an equilateral triangle. From there, you will want to look at the connections of numbers through six points which construct an irregular hexagram. You will want to make sure you follow the order below as the points have to be followed in this order.

1. number 1 connects to 4
2. number 4 connects to 2
3. number 2 connects to 8
4. number 8 connects to 5
5. number 5 connects to 7
6. number 7 connects to 1

When looking at the lines within the Enneagram, you will find that there are arrows which lead you to the following number.

9 Types + 27 Subtypes

You should never think that your personality will fall under just one type of personality. In fact, you will find pieces of your personality in all of the other personalities. However, you should also find the primary number associated with your personality. This number will represent the biggest part of your personality. Remember, the Enneagram is meant to take you out of a box, not put you into one. This is why your personality will be scattered throughout the diagram, but you will have one primary number.

In this section, I will run through the nine types and 27 subtypes that can form your personality. I will not go through these types and subtypes in detail within this section. Instead, the following chapters will be dedicated to each one of the nine types, where I will further discuss the types, subtypes, and other factors in detail.

The nine personality types of the Enneagram are as follows (Berkers, n.d.):

1. The Perfectionist
2. The Helper
3. The Achiever
4. The Individualist
5. The Investigator
6. The Loyalist

7. The Enthusiast
8. The Protector
9. The Mediator

There are a total of 27 subtypes within these nine personality types. There are three main categories that hold these subtypes. These categories are social, self-preservation, and one-on-one (Cloete, n.d.).

The social category focuses on how we get along with other people and our social instincts. It outlines how we maintain relationships and how we work with others. The social category also focuses on how we strive to do the best we can for other people (Cloete, n.d.).

The self-preservation category focuses on how well we preserve our body and mind. It relates to the ways we manage stress and other life events. It is the category that focuses on our emotions. This category looks at ways for us to do our best when it comes to preserving ourselves mentally, physically, and emotionally (Cloete, n.d.).

The one-on-one category focuses on the legacies we want to leave for future generations. Everyone, whether it is within your family or in the world, wants to be remembered when they leave this earth. This category focuses on how we take control of these types of situations. It further dives into our more personal one-on-one relationships with people and environmental factors. Through this category, we can determine what we want to leave behind and how we want to do our best while still on this earth (Cloete, n.d.).

Each personality type has one subtype within the social, self-preservation, and one-on-one category. To gain a better understanding of this, as it is complex, I will list each personality type with its category and subtype below. I will go into each subtype in detail later.

1. The Perfectionist

Social: Not adaptable

Self-preservation: Worry

One-on-one: Zeal

2. The Helper

Social: Ambition

Self-preservation: Privilege

One-on-one: Seduction

3. The Achiever

Social: Prestige

Self-preservation: Security

One-on-one: Charisma

4. The Individualist

Social: Shame

Self-preservation: Tenacity

One-on-one: Competition

5. The Investigator

Social: Totem

Self-preservation: Castle

One-on-one: Confident

6. The Loyalist

Social: Duty

Self-preservation: Warmth

One-on-one: Intimidation

7. The Enthusiast

Social: Sacrifice

Self-preservation: Network

One-on-one: Fascination

8. The Protector

Social: Solidarity

Self-preservation: Satisfaction

One-on-one: Possession

9. The Mediator

Social: Participation

Self-preservation: Appetite

One-on-one: Fusion

Center Points

Beyond the numbers and lines, the diagram is also divided into three triads or centers, which are heart, head, and body. These centers will further develop your personality by explaining your go-to emotions.

1. Heart Center

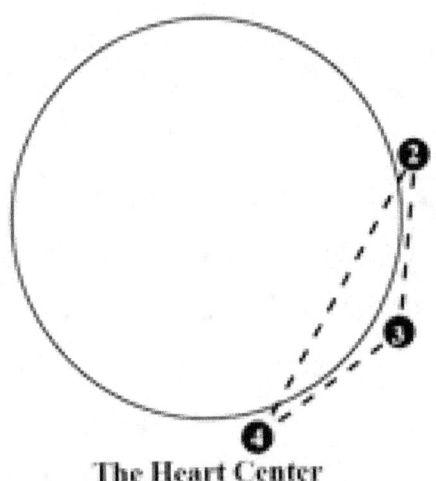

The Heart Center

The heart center focuses on numbers four, three, and two. Because the heart is often thought to be the leader of truth and emotions, these numbers represent someone who is usually more sensitive and strongly believes that we have to be honest about who we are. People who fall into the heart center feel a strong connection to the truth.

The go-to emotion for the heart center is shame. They are very concerned with their image and how other people view them. In fact, they are never truly happy with themselves unless they are able to see themselves through another person's eyes.

Like with the other two centers, the heart center has its strengths and weaknesses, however, these strengths and weaknesses will be determined based on which personality type you have. For example, type four's strengths will be different from type two's ("Heart Triad," n.d.).

Wing Points

The wing points are the parts of your personality which spread out to your two adjacent personality types (Cloete, n.d.). While these two types are not as big as your main personality type, they are important because they will balance out your personality. For instance, if you have a point four personality type, your adjacent type might be a point three. These other types are sometimes known to contradict a person's personality but are important, so we can completely understand the whole of someone's personality. In fact, this is why there are tests and theories like the Enneagram. Not only does it allow us to get to know ourselves better, but it can help people, such as psychologists, who are trying to get to know us so they can help us too.

The question that a lot of people ask is whether we all have one wing or two wings. While this has brought on some controversy, many people believe that we do have two wings. Each point adjacent to our main personality type is one of our wings. Therefore, if you have a type nine personality, your wings will be type one and type eight. But, other people state this is not true and everyone has only one wing. There are other people who state that your wings are not specific to a certain personality type. They believe that because our personality has pieces from every number, then we have our main type and every other type is a wing to our personality, meaning we would have eight wings.

One important note to make about having different wings is that some wings are more dominant than others. If you haven't taken the Enneagram test yet, you will notice that when you get your results, they are laid out in a graph. This graph starts with your main personality as the strongest and then lists the other types of personalities from strongest to weakest. Most results will list all nine personality types.

Lines

One of the hardest parts of the Enneagram theory for people to understand is the lines within the theory. While I discussed the lines before, such as how they connect to the point, I will take this time to give you a bit more information on what the lines mean.

These lines are called the lines of influence or lines of movement (Cloete, n.d.). They are the way you will trace your personality through the Enneagram. Even though we have a main personality type, we can move around between the lines. Our main type will remain the same, however, the situations we go through in life and other factors will influence our journey on the lines throughout the Enneagram.

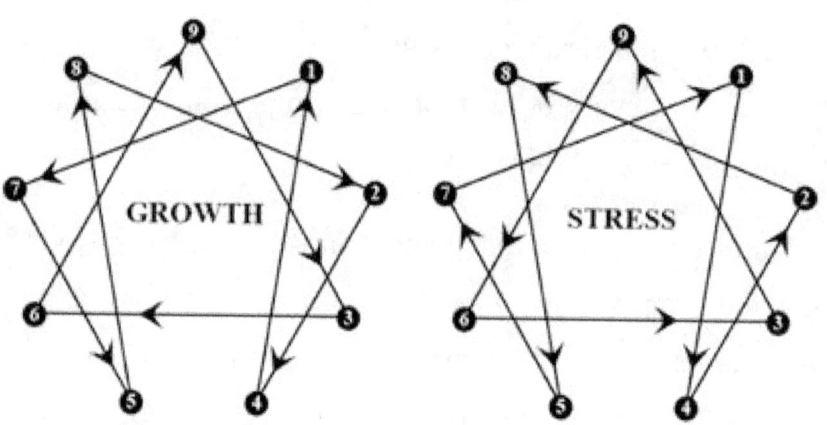

There are two types of lines. There is the line of stress and the line of growth. When you look at your main personality type on the Enneagram, you will see two lines with arrows. One arrow will be pointing away from your number type, which is called the line of growth. The other arrow will be pointing towards your number type and this is referred to as the line of stress.

When you think of the line of growth, you can think of releasing yourself from your unhealthy personality types. This is the line which moves us towards healthier parts of a personality. While we move along this line, we will release our stresses in life and move towards self-actualization (Cloete, n.d.).

The line of stress is the opposite of the line of growth. This line focuses on how we feel when we are under pressure or stressed. Often, these instances will make us pick up unhealthy lifestyle habits. At the same time, we can work to change the negatives into positives, which will often help balance us out as individuals (Cloete, n.d.).

Levels of Integration

Levels of integration are also known as levels of integration. Within each personality type, there are other pieces which make up the personality. These are similar to your behaviors, motivations, and attitude. Basically, these are the pieces which help make up your whole personality, similar to how pieces of the puzzle come together to create the whole puzzle.

When you start to understand these levels, you will come to realize that when people are changing, such as feeling more relaxed one moment and then anxious the next, they are going through different levels within their personality.

There are three levels of integration, which are healthy, average, and unhealthy (Cloete, n.d.). When people exhibit an unhealthy level of integration, they let their fears or other emotions control them. When people are at an average level of integration, the core problem is still a driving force in their behavior, however, they are able to let go of some core issues. When people are at a healthy level of integration, they can let go of the core emotions as they understand why these are occurring. This helps them move on, so they can find a healthier way to manage life stresses and situations. In a sense, they move beyond the limitations they believed they had.

Within these levels of integration are other levels and numbers associated with each level. Each level has three numbers, which correlate to how well the personality performs within its level of integration. These smaller levels are as follows:

In the healthy level, you can be a level one, two or three. Level one is at the level of a libertarian. Level two is at the level of psychological capacity and level three is at the level of social value ("How The System Works," n.d.).

In the average level, you can be a level four, five, or six. Level four is the level representing social role or imbalance. Level five is at the level of interpersonal control. Level six is at the level of overcompensation ("How The System Works," n.d.).

In the unhealthy level, you can be a level seven, eight, or nine. Level seven is a level of violation. Level eight is at the level of compulsion and obsession. Level nine is at the level of pathological destructiveness ("How The System Works," n.d.).

Benefits of the Enneagram

People often turn to the Enneagram to learn more about their personality for many reasons. While some people are curious about their personality type, other people want to know so they can better understand themselves or another person. Psychologists and other professionals often use the Enneagram to help them better understand their patients.

There are several benefits which can come from the Enneagram. Not only can this theory and test benefit people on an individual level, but also as a group. Furthermore, the Enneagram can also benefit people on an organizational level.

Individual Level Benefits

- Help people understand why they are dealing with certain behavioral or emotional problems.
- Help people gain insight into their personality so they can understand themselves better.
- The Enneagram can help increase a person's confidence and motivation.
- The Enneagram can help increase a person's compassion for others.
- People can start to understand their previous behavioral patterns.
- The Enneagram can help people grow in general as they begin to understand their personality better.

Group Level Benefits

- The Enneagram can help decrease conflict within a group.
- It can also help each group member understand where another group member stands, why people act in certain ways, and where each member's strengths and weaknesses are.
- The Enneagram can help improve business processes.
- It can strengthen communication between team members, which will enhance other areas of the group.

Organizational Level Benefits

- The Enneagram can help limit the political atmosphere of an organization.
- It can improve the organization's leadership as a whole.
- The Enneagram can help the organization improve the emotions and fears associated with change.

The Enneagram is so much more than a diagram with lines, numbers, and arrows. It can also do more than to explain a person's personality. As you can see in the benefits above, the Enneagram can help people advance in many areas of their personal and professional life. Furthermore, the Enneagram can continue to help you as you develop through life's different stages.

Chapter 2: The Perfectionist

The first type of personality is the perfectionist, also often called the reformer. Every personality type has a set of words which accurately describe the personality. While you will always want to read through your personality type description, you can also gain an idea of your personality through these few words. For the perfectionist, the descriptive words are perfectionistic, self-controlled, purposeful, and principled.

What is the Perfectionist

When people think of the word perfectionist, they automatically think of a person who is driven, controlling, and needs to make sure everything is always right. While all of this is true about this personality type, like with all other personalities, there are levels of integration. These levels give a range of how healthy or unhealthy a person's personality is. For example, someone with a perfectionist personality who is at an unhealthy level won't listen to someone who contradicts what he or she believes. However, if the type two personality is at a healthy level, then the perfectionist personality is tolerant, accepting, and understands that while he or she wants to be as perfect as possible, perfection is not possible to achieve ("Type One," n.d.).

The true meaning of someone with a type one personality is that they have a very clear concept of what is right and wrong. They understand rules and ethics and think they should be followed thoroughly. At the same time, they want to see positive change and will do what they feel they need to do in order to make this change happen ("Type One," n.d.).

People with a type one personality have a strong fear of making mistakes. This is why they often take more time in completing a task. They need to make sure they are doing everything as perfectly as they can so mistakes will be limited. They often feel like everything needs to be in a certain order and can maintain high standards. Some of their flaws include not having patience, becoming too controlling, and resentful ("Type One," n.d.).

The perfectionists' biggest fear is corruption. While there are many reasons for this, one of the biggest is that they see corruption as unorderly and lacking control. When there is corruption, ethical standards are not followed and the conditions are not improving ("Type One," n.d.).

The biggest desire for a perfectionist is to be the best person possible. The perfectionist wants to be a good person overall, even if he or she exhibits personality traits of impatience and withdraws from other people. These traits are often used as a defense mechanism to help the type one manage their perfectionist traits. Type one also wants to see a well-balanced world around them.

Some people who are known to have type one personalities are Katherine Hepburn, Maggie Smith, Tina Fey, Hilary Clinton, Michelle Obama, Joan of Arc, Nelson Mandela, Jerry Seinfeld, Prince Charles, Jimmy Carter, and Kate Middleton ("Type One," n.d.).

People who have type one personality feel the need to have a mission to accomplish. Not only do they have a mission to focus on, but they will also do whatever they can to fulfill this mission. At the same time, they feel the need to justify their actions to themselves. They will do this by asking themselves questions to why this mission is important and conducting research. If they decide their actions are justified, they become very passionate and work hard to make improvements.

The type one personality won't often let themselves stray from their mission or responsibilities ("Type One," n.d.). Because of this, they can become resentful towards others or the conditions. This can often make the perfectionist seem controlling and unable to adapt to his or her surroundings. However, this is generally not true. The problem is because the perfectionist is struggling to improve conditions, they become frustrated and act out aggressively or become resentful. This is the way many type one personalities manage their struggles, mistakes, and the realization that the situation is uncontrollable.

Level of Integration

As stated earlier, all personalities have a level of integration. These consist of three different levels, which are healthy, average, and unhealthy. Within these levels are smaller levels which range from one to nine. The healthy level consists of levels one through three. The moderate level consists of levels four through six, and the unhealthy level consists of levels seven through nine. Level one means a type one personality at its best. Of course, the level will either increase or decrease depending on how the type one personality deals with his or her environmental situations. This means that when a personality reaches an unhealthy level, such as nine, he or she is at their worst.

Healthy Level

When a type one personality is at level one, they are performing at their best. They have found ways to manage their stress during situations that keeps them from becoming too aggressive and controlling. While they don't always manage everything perfectly, they realize that this is fine because perfection doesn't truly exist. However, this won't keep them from continuing to try. They also realize that they cannot control various environmental factors or what other people do. Therefore, they feel calmer when things don't go as planned. They think that as long as they perform their best, they are successful. They know that as long as they are mindful of the moment, they will be able to see and give others the truth (Cloete, n.d.).

Perfectionists at level two healthy level continue to work to improve themselves as they know they can be better. At this level, the type one will know what is right from wrong. Furthermore, they will understand ethics in all environments, from a working standpoint to religious ethics. They remain strong when it comes to their own moral values and strive to become self-disciplined. They are also very responsible, mature, and rational about circumstances ("Type One," n.d.).

A level three type one is at a lower healthy level. They still maintain a healthy way of keeping their aggression controlled in most situations. They strive to continue to do their best. They are rational and very concerned about ethics and making sure they are followed. These levels tend to make great teachers because of the belief that they have a higher purpose to make sure others see the truth. They also believe in fairness, even within state and federal laws ("Type One," n.d.).

Average Level

The highest level for a type one under the average level is a level four. People who are at this level can't always control their behaviors over their emotions. They believe that it is up to them to improve society's conditions, which is a belief they are very passionate about. Unlike the perfectionists at a healthy level, they don't always think rationally about their actions and can sometimes find themselves resentful or aggressive. This usually is shown through telling people that what they are doing is wrong and explaining how things should be instead (Cloete, n.d.).

A perfectionist, who is at a level five, is often considered a "workaholic." They strive to make sure everything has an order, including their emotions. While they do tend to become overly emotional, especially when they make mistakes, they do their best to keep these emotions hidden from other people. Like most perfectionists, they are known to have a strong sense of what is right and wrong, however, they can also be impressionable. This can cause them to follow people who won't help them achieve their order and in turn they will make mistakes. When this happens, the type one can become resentful (Cloete, n.d.).

A level six perfectionist has strong opinions and is highly critical of other people and themselves. Type one personalities at the lowest average level don't watch their reactions as well as other perfectionists do. Therefore, they are often deemed to be angry and impatient. Furthermore, they are known to scold people who they believe are doing wrong. These perfectionists like to have things done their way and don't believe that any other way is correct (Cloete, n.d.).

Unhealthy Level

An unhealthy level for a type one personality is a level seven. People who are in this category are often referred to as bullies. They are people who believe that no one else is right, except for them. In fact, some people refer to perfectionists at this level as narcissists. They can become very angry and lack patience when things aren't as they should be ("Type One," n.d.).

A level eight perfectionist often becomes so focused on what wrong things other people are doing that they lose track of what wrong things they are doing themselves. When this happens, they can find themselves doing the opposite of what they think is right. They tend to be very illogical thinkers and can have trouble problem-solving as they tend to do what they feel is right instead of what is actually right. They don't have a clear sense of morals and values as much as other type one personalities above them do ("Type One," n.d.).

A level nine represents a type one being at their lowest level of integration. They struggle in several areas for various reasons. Some perfectionists at this level are diagnosed with various mental illnesses, such as severe depression and obsessive-compulsive disorder. Unfortunately, suicidal thoughts and suicide are also high at this level (Cloete, n.d.).

Subtypes of the Perfectionist

Social Category is Non-Adaptable

Perfectionists are non-adaptable because they follow the rules and morals of what is right. They also believe that it is their job to make things right, if they see them as wrong, and are not typically flexible in this area. One of their biggest motivations to make things right is to make sure there is fairness (Cloete, n.d.).

Self-Preservation Category is Worry

Perfectionists spend a lot of time worrying because they want to make sure everything they do and everything that is around them is right. Therefore, they not only worry about their actions but the actions of others. This can cause them to feel anxious, especially when they believe that things aren't going as planned. Part of this is because they need to make sure they are well-prepared for their current situations. This not only includes making sure everything is in an orderly fashion, but also noticing every single detail which other people may miss (Cloete, n.d.).

One-on-One Category is Zeal

Zeal is known as a countertype. Depending on the healthy, average, and unhealthy level of a type one personality, it will determine how well they manage their personal relationships. Because many believe they are right, they feel authorized to tell others they are wrong. This can often cause all sorts of conflict when it comes to close relationships (Cloete, n.d.).

Relationships with Other Types

Type one is compatible with every other personality type. No matter what type they come in contact with, they can work with the individual. Of course, each personality will bring its own positivity and challenges to the relationship. For example, when it comes to a type one working with another type one, they will often run into conflict because they both strongly believe that they know only one of them is right. Therefore, if they don't agree on something, they will struggle to find any type of happy-medium. Perfectionists are very compatible with types nine, two, five, seven, and eight. They will struggle more with types one, three, four, and six. However, all this will also depend on the level of integration a type one associates with, along with the level of integration the other personality type associates with ("Relationships (Type Combinations)," n.d.).

Wing Types

The two wing personalities for the perfectionist are type nine and type two. Both of these wings will give the perfectionist positives and challenges. The positives for type nine are their drive, helping perfectionists become more relaxed, becoming more considerate of other people, and understanding that other people can also be right. One of the challenges that type nine brings to type one is that they might neglect situations which are difficult and in turn self-neglect.

The positives which type two brings to the perfectionist are taking care of themselves, helping others, and having compassion for other people. The challenges type two can bring to type one are the feeling of being taken advantage of and becoming overly sensitive to what other people think about them (Cloete, n.d.).

Center Point

A type one personality falls under the body center (Cloete, n.d.). If you have a type one personality, you will internalize your anger. People who have type one personality are very self-critical and often hard on themselves to a fault. They don't criticize themselves harshly because they lack criticism, they do this because they don't want to show their anger externally. In fact, they often try their hardest to make sure they don't show anger towards other people.

Type one's strengths:

- Hard-working
- Honest
- Independent
- Reliable
- Accountable

Type one's weaknesses:

- Rigidness
- Overly-critical
- Judgmental
- Resentful

How to Grow Personally

Whether you believe you are at the healthiest level of integration or close to the highest, there is always room for personal growth in your professional and personal life. Below are several pieces of advice which can help you grow as someone with a type one personality.

Keep the Right Mindset

While this will take time and how much time depends on what level you are currently at. Of course, the higher the level, the more time it will take. When I talk about the right mindset, I am talking about several characteristics, such as patience for others, remaining calm, and keeping your emotions in check. Furthermore, most type one personalities think they are always right, which can cause them to become emotional if people don't follow their ways or prove that they are wrong.

Perfectionists are known to be great teachers. However, they often struggle with teaching because they lack patience and consideration for people who do something wrong. But, if you have the right mindset, you will find that you can be an exceptional teacher; you will just have to make sure you have the patience, are able to deal with people who make mistakes, realize that you are not always right, and also realize that perfectionism is not completely possible. While reaching all these factors might seem impossible to you, especially if you have a lower level of integration, you do possess the motivation and drive to make sure you succeed if you become passionate about acquiring the right mindset.

You will want to remain calm. Perfectionists often struggle with keeping their emotions in check. Many perfectionists struggle with keeping their emotions in check because they are highly rigid about how things need to be done. Their primary emotion is anger, which means that they will show more anger than any other emotion. This can cause more problems within the issues already established. Therefore, the calmer you are able to remain, the more you will succeed in keeping your emotions, especially anger, in check. Once you are able to control your anger, you will find it is easier to control other emotions (Cloete, n.d.).

Chapter 3: The Helper

Type two personality is known as the helper and the giver. This personality type is one which focuses on helping others. Some of the primary words used to describe the helper are people-pleaser, demonstrative, possessive, and generous. The stress line for the helper shifts from a type two to a type eight, while the growth line shifts from a type two to a type four.

What is the Helper?

Stevie Wonder, Danny Glover, Martin Sheen, Elizabeth Taylor, and Richard Thomas (John boy Walton) are all considered to have a type two personality. People who have this personality type are typically warm and caring individuals. Not only are they generous but they are highly compassionate and don't tend to pass judgment. They are driven by their need to help others and can often be found in professions such as non-profits and volunteering at soup kitchens ("Type Two," n.d).

A type two's biggest desire is to be loved while their biggest fear is the feeling of being unwanted or unloved. In fact, one of the biggest reasons they focus on helping people is to fulfill this desire. They believe that the more they help people, the more people will enjoy their company and care about them. It is this feeling that makes helpers take so much time out of their day to make sure they are fulfilling their mission of helping other people.

People quickly see that type two personalities have big hearts. Therefore, they are drawn to helpers. Unfortunately, this can also cause problems because there are many people who are more interested in taking advantage of helpers. For many type two personalities, this becomes a problem because they don't often have the courage to defend themselves against people who take advantage of them. While some are able to defend themselves, many others continue to help people because they fear that people will not like them if they don't help..

Individuals with a type two personality are similar to a sponge. They tend to soak up emotions from other people, which can cause them to feel overwhelmed by all the different emotions. If they don't know how to release these emotions, they can be prone to emotional outbursts as this allows them to relieve the pressure. Because of this, it is important for them to find a balance between feeling loved by other people and loving themselves. No matter how much love you feel from someone else, it will never substitute self-love.

Levels of Integration

Healthy Level

A level one type two is the best level that you can reach. These types of people don't ever think that they should be rewarded for helping. People who reach this level are known to be selfless and help people because they feel true unconditional love for others, even those who have wronged them or others in the past. They believe that it is a privilege to be accepted by other people and be a part of their lives (Cloete, n.d.).

A level two type two is similar to a level one, however, these types sometimes believe that they should receive some help back. While they are extremely warm, compassionate, and caring individuals, they also hold more realistic expectations of how people can take advantage of them. However, they don't always act when they think they are being taken advantage of ("Type Two," n.d.).

A level three type two tends to take care of themselves as much as they take care of other people. They like to maintain a good balance, however, if it comes down to either help themselves or another person, they will help the other person first. Like the higher type two personalities, they are very nurturing, warm, caring, and generous. They believe that everyone has an ultimate good about them (Cloete, n.d.).

Average Level

A level four type two will have a lot of helpful qualities and good intentions. They don't often feel that they are entitled to help from other people. However, they also brag about how helpful they are. They believe that people should acknowledge their behavior and reward them. However, they don't often look for materialistic rewards, they would rather receive a reward through praise (Cloete, n.d.).

A level five type two personalities expect a return from the people they help. Those at a level five also tend to feel so strongly towards helping people that they can come off as more pushy than helpful (Cloete, n.d.). They don't fully understand the line between being helpful and becoming overly helpful.

A level six type two personality can also become overbearing when they are helping others (Cloete, n.d.). They believe that they do deserve rewards, however, they are not always open about this belief. They feel that they are irreplaceable and have a strong sense of self-importance.

Unhealthy Level

When a helper is at a level seven, they can often be manipulative. While they still like to help other people, they also feel more entitled to help (Cloete, n.d.). For example, if a type two personality helps you with raking your lawn, he or she will tell you how much you owe him or her the next time they need or want something. Unlike healthy level type two's, this unhealthy level will often think that he or she shouldn't complete any actions for free. In a sense, level seven type two's always want something back, a reward of sorts, for their helpful behavior.

A level eight type two is similar to a level seven but often feels entitled to any type of favor they want from someone else (Cloete, n.d.). These favors can come in the form of money, house work, or sexual activities. Someone who ranks at level eight for a type two personality is generally not shy about asking what they want. Furthermore, they don't possess the warm and caring personality that the majority of type two personalities do when they are asking for help.

A level nine type two is the lowest level that a type two personality can have. Similar to the other unhealthy levels, they feel highly entitled to favors and jobs performed by other people (Cloete, n.d.). However, they will also justify their behavior and the way they treat people because of the helpful nature of their personality. They believe that because they treat people with kindness, they are able to act towards a person how they wish.

Subtypes of the Helper

Social Category is Ambition

Type two personalities have a lot of ambition and can often be seen taking on leadership roles. They like to feel like they are important and needed, therefore, they will find people and organizations who need them. Because of their caring and helpful personality, people are quickly attracted to them, which easily helps them engage groups of people. This can also allow the helper to get what they want out of the groups, such as completing tasks or getting more help from others (Cloete, n.d.).

However, type two personalities often feel uncomfortable when they are alone. This happens for several reasons, one being that they feel they are not doing whatever they can to help someone. Therefore, many professionals agree that helpers will use their personality in order to block out their uncomfortable feelings. The busier they are, the less likely they will be able to feel what they don't want to feel (Cloete, n.d.).

Self-Preservation Category is Privilege

This is the countertype of type two. In fact, they are often mistaken to be a type seven personality. A type two can often cause other personalities to feel like they need to be protected because of their helpful nature. Because of this, type two is often considered to be a little child-like and shy. They don't mind feeling like they are being protected, however, they also don't want to become too dependent on someone else. They feel that their sense of self-protection is a privilege, so they treat it with care. Furthermore, they have a big fear of rejection, which makes them feel like they have to protect themselves more than someone else would (Cloete, n.d.).

One-on-One Category is Seduction

Type two personalities are very giving, compassionate, and thought to be extremely selfless, however, this doesn't mean that they don't want to feel important to someone. No matter what level a type two personality is, whether healthy, average, or unhealthy, they still feel a need to receive compassion and love from someone. Therefore, when type two personalities get into an intimate relationship, they start to feel this connection very strongly. They will often use the caring and loving parts of their personality towards their partner so they can feel these emotions back.

Once the type two personality gets into a very close relationship, they can start to feel very passionate. Of course, this passion comes with positives and negatives. For example, one positive is they will begin to feel more comfortable and trust their partner. However, one negative is they will start to have trouble taking no for an answer. In fact, they might find it hard to set and follow limits (Cloete, n.d.).

Relationships with Other Types

Type two personalities tend to get along with type one and type three the best because these personalities are type two's wings. However, they also get along with generally any type of personality. But, of course, they will struggle with some personalities more than others. For example, type two and type five struggle with getting along. While they will eventually get along, type two views type five as a challenging personality that is often difficult to form a relationship with ("Relationships (Type Combinations)," n.d.).

Some of these types are better off as friends and co-workers rather than to be in a romantic relationship. For example, type four and type two get along exceptionally well and often create a very warm and compassionate relationship. However, they make better friends than romantic partners.

Wing Types

The two wings for type two personality are type one and type three. Both of these wings not only help type two to manage their personality better, but also involves challenges. When it comes to positives, the type one will bring more balance to the type two by having them help everyone and not their favorite people. Furthermore, type one helps them establish boundaries so people don't consistently take the type two for granted. Type one can also help type two improve their environment. When it comes to challenges, type one can make type two have unrealistic expectations, become too hard on themselves for mistakes, become sensitive to criticism, and cause them to neglect themselves (Cloete, n.d.).

The type three personality can provide type two advantages by helping them with their focus, self-esteem, and the ability to adapt to other people and their surroundings. The challenges that type two faces with a type three wing is the act of neglecting themselves because they become too focused on their work and become selective when it comes to helping people (Cloete, n.d.).

Center Point

If you have a type two personality, you will sit under the heart center point and externalize your feelings of shame (Cloete, n.d.). This is often what makes you become the best person you can be, which is why you are often seen as helpful and supportive. In a sense, you use your shame in order to create a better person and help others. This provides you with an image of yourself as being needed and well-liked, which makes you feel better about your shame.

Type two's strengths:

- Helpful
- Generous
- Supportive
- Caring
- Relationships
- Sensitive

Type two's weaknesses:

- Dependent
- Demanding
- Prideful
- Privileged
- Intrusive

How to Grow Personally

Remember to Ask People What They Need

A type two personality wants to help people in any way possible. Because of this, they often forget to ask the person what type of help they really need or want. Sometimes people don't want to receive the help you are giving them, which means you aren't really helping them at all. It is important for other people, and yourself, to make sure that you are using your energy on the people who really want the help. Don't be afraid to ask them if you can help them in any way. If people really need the help, they will let you know. If they tell you that they don't need your help, just let them know that you are available if they ever do. Often, when people know that you are available to help them is all they need to hear to feel loved and cared about (Cloete, n.d.).

Be Conscious of Your Motives

As stated above, there are a few levels of type two personalities that expect certain things in return and start to feel entitled to being treated well because of the way they treat others. This is an example of poor interior motives, which is something that you should improve on if you begin to feel this way. While everyone has the internal feeling of wanting to receive some of the help and compassion they give to others, when you start to feel like you deserve this compassion and love because of your actions, you should take a step back and rethink your motives. You want to help other people because it's a part of your personality. You want to be compassionate to others because you hold a special personality that strongly advocates compassion. You want to use these important pieces of your personality to strengthen the lives of others and not cause harm (Cloete, n.d.).

Don't Forget About Yourself

You might think that you deserve rewards because you are forgetting to take care of yourself. This is often a weakness for someone with a type two personality. No matter what personality you have, it is important to make sure that you take time for yourself and give yourself the care you need, so you can live a happy and healthy life. Type two personalities often forget to take care of themselves because they are so fixated on taking care of other people. However, this can harm you in the end. Therefore, it is important to make sure to give yourself some care and pampering time just as you would for anyone else. Doing so will allow you to spread your unconditional love to others easier (Cloete, n.d.).

Chapter 4: The Achiever

The stress line for type three personality runs from point three to point nine and its growth line runs from three to point six. The primary words used to describe an achiever are driven, adaptable, image-conscious, and excelling. Some famous achievers are O.J. Simpson, Paul McCartney, Madonna, Muhammad Ali, Will Smith, Bill Clinton, and Michael Jordan ("Type Three," n.d).

What is the Achiever?

Type three personalities are known to be very driven. They are considered workaholics and tend to be concerned about what other people think of them. They are known to be ambitious, energetic, diplomatic, and always looking at ways they can advance in their careers in life ("Type Three," n.d.).

An achiever's biggest fear is the feeling of being worthless internally and externally. Therefore, they will strive to become the best person possible. They want to do their best in their career field. Achievers also want other people to see how well they do in their career and other aspects of their life.

An achiever's desire is to feel worthwhile and valued. They often feel this way when they continue to reach their goals and remain ambitious to do their best. In fact, because they are so ambitious, people often look up to them. Many people believe that achievers are some of the most inspirational people because of everything they accomplish.

For achievers, there are many things that help them define their success. They use their status in their careers and their personal lives. They use their popularity as a way to measure success. At the same time, they also use their relationships with their friends, family, and co-workers to define their success ("Type Three," n.d.).

Most achievers tend to be considered popular because people want to be associated with them. Not only do they look up to them, but many other personalities believe that achievers can also help them accomplish their goals in life. In fact, out of all the personality types, the achiever is known to be the most well-liked.

However, the need to be successful is not just to fulfill their needs in life. In fact, most think that they won't get attention from other people unless they are successful. Like any other personality, type three wants to feel like they are needed and accepted by others. Therefore, they use their drive to become successful, believing this is how they will acquire this feeling from others.

Because of this, people with this type of personality can often forget about what they want in life. In fact, when they do is take a step back and realize they are neglecting themselves, because they have no idea what they truly want to get out of their life. This can lead type three personalities to a crossroad. While they want to continue to be successful, so other people give them what they desire most, they also realize they can't continue to neglect themselves. This is when a lot of issues arise for the achiever as they begin to strive to find a balance.

Levels of Integration

Healthy Level

The best level an achiever can reach is the first level. Achievers who are at a level one are completely honest with their accomplishments, which are often astounding to many people. They work hard and always put in as much effort as they can in everything they do. They are also known to be very charitable, gentle, and self-accepting. They have found a balance between showing people their success and taking care of themselves. Furthermore, they are known to be non-judgmental and want to help others achieve success as well (Cloete, n.d.).

An achiever at level two has high self-esteem and knows their value. However, they often don't admit their value to other people because this might make them seem arrogant. It's at the level two when achievers start paying attention to other people's opinions of them. So they can continue their success and become the best person they can be. They believe that people have to see them this way. Therefore, they don't believe in bragging about their accomplishments. In fact, they are known to be shy about what they accomplish in their lives. People see achievers at level two as very adaptable, charming, and generous (Cloete, n.d.).

A level three achiever is constantly focusing on doing the best they can for themselves and other people. They are often seen as a role model because of their drive and ability to succeed. However, most level three achievers do not know their true worth when it comes to their career and personal life. One reason for this is because they are always trying to better themselves. Therefore, no matter what they do, they think that they can do it even better. However, they do realize they are successful people as they are proud of the achievements they accomplish (Cloete, n.d.).

Average Level

At level four, achievers believe that their self-worth depends on the achievements they have made in life. They will continue to push themselves to do the best they can. At this point, achievers tend to forget about their own emotions and mentality when it comes to accomplishing their goals. While they are seen by others as being incredibly successful, they never believe they are truly that successful and continue to work harder. One reason for this is because the fear of failure is intense for a level four. They are constantly worried about how they failed or how they could fail, which gives them more energy to succeed (Cloete, n.d.).

An achiever at level five starts to become more worried about how they appear to other people. They will often ask people what they think or how they feel about them. When they are told, they take the person's answer to heart and do what they can to continue to improve themselves. At this level, achievers start to forget about what they want to completely focusing on what other people think they should do or what other people want to see them accomplish. Level five achievers begin to lose touch with their reality and forget about how they need to care for themselves first (Cloete, n.d.).

At level six, an achiever starts to promote themselves as much as possible. They spend a lot of their time bragging about their accomplishments and observing what other people think about what they accomplished. People at a level six also tend to lie about what they have accomplished because they need to make sure that they sound better than they really are. It is at this level they start to exhibit signs of narcissism and are believed to be very arrogant (Cloete, n.d.).

Unhealthy Level

At a level seven, an achiever's fear of being forgotten becomes so strong that they will do whatever they can to make sure people don't forget about them or their achievements. At this stage, they have to make sure that people continue to believe they are superior. In fact, at this level, they want people to think that they could never be as good as the achiever (Cloete, n.d.).

When an achiever is at level eight, they can become dishonest and manipulative. This is because they will start to believe they need to cover up their mistakes at all costs. This is also when they start to become jealous of other people who they believe are doing better then they are. In order to remain on top, they will start to deceive people into thinking that they are better than anyone else (Cloete, n.d.).

The lowest level for an achiever is level nine. At this level, achievers exhibit signs of psychopathic behavior or are considered to be narcissistic. Achievers who are a level nine will do whatever it takes to make sure they are the best and people believe they are the best, even if it means hurting someone in order to remain on top. Achievers who are a level nine will ruin someone else's happiness in order to gain what they want and accomplish their goals, or at least give people the illusion that they accomplished their goals (Cloete, n.d.).

Subtypes of the Achiever

Social Category is Prestige

Type three personalities are very concerned about their outward appearance. In fact, they sometimes become so concerned that they will cheat and lie in order to make themselves look more successful than they are. They are competitive by nature and will do what they can in order to gain the spotlight. At the same time, they are very talented and while they can be competitive, they also work well in groups. In fact, they are known to adjust to their social settings, which is one reason they are successful (Cloete, n.d.).

Self-Preservation Category is Security

Security is the countertype to the achiever. While they like to know what other people think of them and often base their success on their outward appearance, they don't want people to believe they care about what other people think. In a sense, achievers like to keep this a secret (Cloete, n.d.).

One-on-One Category is Charisma

Achievers compete for the spotlight, but at the same time, they can be very rational about the spotlight they get. Part of this is because of their security and not wanting to show that they want to be in the spotlight. Another part of this is because when achievers are at a healthy level of integration, they realize that it's not necessary that people know about all their achievements.

Furthermore, achievers are known to maintain good relationships. In fact, many people think that type three personalities are very supportive because they want to see other people succeed as well. This is especially true when achievers work in groups. Achievers often follow the belief that if the people they hang out with are successful, they too will become successful (Cloete, n.d.).

Relationships with Other Types

How well a type three gets along with other personalities will depend on the developmental level of the achiever. A type three who is around a level seven to nine will struggle to get along with a lot of other personalities because they tend to have high narcissistic tendencies and believe they are better than everyone else. However, for achievers who are in a more healthy or average level will be able to get along with almost any other personality type. However, the personality type that most achievers will deem a challenge is type six. However, they are able to work well together ("Relationships (Type Combinations)," n.d.).

Wing Types

The achiever's wings are personality types two and four. In regard to type two, the achiever receives several strengths, such as learning how to balance their work and personal life. Furthermore, type two personality helps type three realize that they can't use people, they have to value their thoughts and beliefs. Because of type two, achievers are able to strengthen their personal relationships, whether they are intimate or not. However, there are also challenges for type three. One of these challenges is that type two can make achievers strive for the approval of others. This can also cause the achievers to feel burnt-out because they work too hard to impress other people and become very critical of themselves when they think people don't value their achievements (Cloete, n.d.).

Type four teaches the achievers to value friendships with others. They help type three realize they have to be true to themselves in order to really achieve the success they want to achieve. At the same time, they help type three reach a sensitivity when it comes to the way other people are feeling. However, this can also become a challenge for achievers. A type four personality can also lead achievers to withdraw from people, which can cause them to become moody or irritated. Furthermore, this can lead them to think that people don't appreciate them and what they have accomplished. When achievers begin to think this way, they start to brag about their achievements and believe that people should be more appreciative and pay more attention to everything they have accomplished. Another negative that the type four wing can bring to a type three is force them to jump into relationships just because they are looking for something that's missing. For example, if a type three doesn't feel appreciated, they will strive to feel appreciation in their intimate relationship (Cloete, n.d.).

Center Point

A type three personality is part of the heart center (Cloete, n.d.). If you have a type three personality, you will understand who you are through the feedback of other people. This is because you are often out of touch with your own feelings, which makes getting a clear sense of who you are, or how well you do on something, difficult. As a type three, you find yourself resenting your feeling of shame, which can lead you to your strengths and weaknesses. For example, you change the shame you feel into success.

Type three's strengths:

- Strive for success
- Enthusiastic
- Practical
- Problem-solving
- Efficient
- Determined
- Competent

Type three's weaknesses:

- Overworked
- Competitive
- Image-driven
- Impatient
- Out of touch with your feelings

How to Grow Personally

Remember to Take Breaks

Because type three personalities are such high achievers and always looking at what they can accomplish next, they often forget to take care of themselves. This can easily wear a person out and cause them to feel emotionally, mentally, and physically exhausted. When this happens, they can easily fall from a level two or three to a level five or six. Therefore, it is essential that achievers remember to take breaks and to make sure they take time to care for their mental and emotional health.

While ambition and dedication to achieve your goals and become successful are great qualities, like any characteristics they can have negative effects. Some of these effects can harm you mentally, emotionally, and physically ("Type Three," n.d.). For example, you can drive yourself into exhaustion or you can start to feel majorly depressed because you do not take care of yourself. Whether it is working too hard or not taking time for yourself, you have to remember that you can only truly succeed if you are fully charged and ready. You don't have to take a lot of time to charge, in fact, just taking a quick break can help you feel recharged.

Remember Your Interests

Because achievers tend to focus so much on what other people think about them, they often forget about their own interests. Instead, they try to show interest in factors that other people find interesting and want them to achieve, even if the type three is not interested. While many achievers will continue to work towards this goal, because they want to show others they can achieve it, they can quickly start to feel a sense of worthlessness or depression because they are not working towards what they want to do ("Type Three," n.d.).

Because of this, it is important to make sure that what you are working towards is what you want to do, and not what someone else wants you to do. You have to have some type of interest in your work or else you will harm yourself mentally and emotionally. Instead of doing what you can to prove your accomplishments to others, you can start working with them. This way, even if you are not fully interested in the task, you are with people who are and by working as a team, you will be able to remain successful.

Be Honest with Yourself

In order to truly be successful, you have to be honest with yourself and everyone else. Don't spend time to inflate your accomplishments. Instead, be honest with them. Let them know what you have really accomplished and what you didn't accomplish. The more realistic you are about your achievements, the more people are going to see you as a role model. People look up to others who are honest. If they find that you are constantly bragging about your accomplishments or lying about what you have completed, they are less likely to see you as successful and someone worth trusting ("Type Three," n.d.).

Chapter 5: The Individualist

The primary words used to describe an individualist are dramatic, expressive, temperamental, and self-absorbed. The growth line for a type four personality moves to a type one personality. The stress line moves from a type four to a type two personality. Some famous people with type four personalities include Johnny Depp, Kate Winslet, Amy Winehouse, Billie Holiday, Judy Garland, Anne Frank, and Hank Williams ("Type Four," n.d.).

What is the Individualist?

Type four personalities are known to be extremely sensitive to what is going on around them. They tend to feel emotions deeply. In fact, most feel emotions on a deeper level than other personalities. Of course, this can cause problems when it comes to a type four because they can have trouble controlling their feelings, which can become overwhelming. Because of this, the individualist will need to use certain techniques, so they can manage the stress of their emotions.

Because of how overwhelming emotions can be, the individualist will withdraw from society. They will usually have a select group of friends they regularly see and talk to, and they tend to withdraw from others. Their overwhelming emotions can also cause them to feel self—pity, melancholy, or become severely depressed. Just because type four personalities tend to withdraw from society, doesn't mean they want to be alone in their life. Unfortunately, because of their lack of social life, they often begin to feel this way which can increase their depression or internal sadness. At the same time, because individualists are concerned about their self-image, they will often become anxious when in a social setting. They are afraid of making a mistake that will cause people to judge them or think that they are socially awkward, which will deter them from social settings ("Type Four," n.d.).

The biggest struggle a type four has in regard to their emotions is letting go of the past. They often feel guilty over mistakes they have made, especially if it negatively affected their self-image. On top of this, they genuinely struggle with letting go of emotions. Therefore, type four personalities can hold on to emotions for years, if not longer.

Their main desire is to feel that they have significance ("Type Four," n.d.). They want to be sure they have an identity in the world and be able to understand themselves. When it comes to their biggest fear, which is also their strongest emotion, they worry about their identity and what special features they have. They want to do something special and become noticed. Therefore, they are often worried about their personal significance and fear that they have none.

The reason why this fear is so extreme for the individualist is because they know they aren't like other people. They believe they are different, which makes them believe that others cannot understand them. While they know they possess unique and one-of-a-kind talents, they also believe that they are uniquely flawed. Because of this, they tend to become more aware of their unique characteristics more than other people. They also make sure to take care of these characteristics more than most people. Individualists believe that their unique characteristics are some of the most important features of their personality ("Type Four," n.d.).

Type four personalities are often motivated when they are able to express their individuality. They also like to see the beauty in the world and will often surround themselves with what they find beautiful. They also receive motivation when they are allowed to take care of themselves before they need to take care of someone else. However, they enjoy knowing that they are about to help other people ("Type Four," n.d.).

Other than becoming overwhelmed with emotions, individualists often think that they are missing something in their life. Unfortunately, they never fully grasp an idea of what they are missing. Therefore, they think it can be a variety of factors and will often try different careers or change aspects of their personality to figure out what is missing ("Type Four," n.d.). For example, some might think they don't have enough friends, so they will start to become more social. Other individualists might think that they are missing a piece of themselves, such as self-confidence, so they will start to increase their confidence.

A couple of the biggest problems individualists face with themselves is their lack of self-esteem and poor self-image. Both of these factors tend to negatively affect individualists in several ways throughout their life. For example, it can be what causes them to become socially withdrawn, not use their talent to its fullest potential, or become afraid to try something new out of fear of what it will do to their self-image. Because of this, they will often compensate by creating an idealized image of themselves. They use this image as someone they want others to see them as. They will also use this imaginary version of themselves to become the best person they can be.

Levels of Integration

Healthy Level

The highest level for an individualist is level one, which means that they are able to let go of their past emotions, realize they have a positive self-image, and are able to take all their life experiences and transform them into something special and valuable. These experiences are able to help them learn and grow, which is what they focus on when they are transforming. They also realize they are very unique and creative people, and are not shy about expressing themselves, whether it is through art, music, or writing (Cloete, n.d.).

At a level two, individualists are known to be extremely gentle, sensitive, and compassionate. They are aware that they internalize feelings deeply and use techniques in order to help themselves manage the feeling of becoming overwhelmed with emotion. They are comfortable with their self-image, but also believe that they still need to improve themselves. Furthermore, they still continue to search for who they really are (Cloete, n.d.).

An individualist who is at a level three, is honest with themselves and others. They are self-aware of their emotions but often overcome their overwhelming feeling with humor. In fact, they are known to not be very serious people because they tend to find humor in almost anything. Even if they think their self-image has drawn on some negativity, they realize that this happens because no one is perfect and people make mistakes. Therefore, they are known to remain true to themselves (Cloete, n.d.).

Average Level

A type four who is at a level four tends to use their creative abilities to overcome their strong feelings. They are also known to be the most romantic individualists. Like others, they focus on creating a beautiful environment around them, even if they have to create a fantasy to do this. They are known to have an active imagination but do their best to remain true to their passionate emotions (Cloete, n.d.).

Individualists who are at a level five tend to take everything personally and have trouble separating what isn't aimed at them and what is. Because of this, they are perceived to be very self-absorbed people but, in reality, they are hypersensitive. They are also very self-conscious and shy, which makes it hard for them to become spontaneous. They are considered to be introverted. They often don't spend a lot of time in social settings because it helps them protect their self-image. Another reason they are introverted is because it allows them to control their emotions better because they are able to out their emotions (Cloete, n.d.).

A type four who is at a level six tends to focus more on self-pity because they realize they are different, which means they cannot live the same way as other people do. Because of this, they will often create a happier and healthier fantasy world. Other people tend to view a level six as self-indulgent and unproductive. At the same time, they are also viewed as dreamers and unique individuals (Cloete, n.d.).

Unhealthy Level

One of the unhealthy levels for a type four is a level seven. At this level, individualists tend to get very angry with themselves, which makes them become socially withdrawn. Because of this, they often struggle with depression. Furthermore, they start to feel ashamed by their overwhelming emotions, which makes them block out their emotions. A level seven will often struggle with daily functioning because they often feel exhausted. Individualists will start to reach this level when their fantasy world fails and they can no longer imagine a happier world for themselves (Cloete, n.d.).

A level eight often starts to feel tormented by their self-image. These individualists usually have very low self-esteem and often blame others for their problems. At this level, individualists tend to hate themselves and think melancholy. They will often push away anyone who tries to help them for several reasons, such as wanting to be alone or feeling like they don't deserve the help (Cloete, n.d.).

The highest level that individualists can reach is a level nine. Type four personalities who reach this level typically have problems with drugs and alcohol as this helps them cope with their morbid thoughts and low self-esteem. They often find themselves contemplating suicide and suffer from various mental diseases such as narcissistic and avoidant personality disorders (Cloete, n.d.).

Subtypes of the Individualist

Social Category is Shame

Shame is the basic emotion for a type four personality. Therefore, this emotion shows up in their daily lives constantly. In fact, they can quickly make themselves feel guilty, which will cause them to also feel ashamed. While they are not competitive, they do like people telling them they are positively influencing other people in society. They like to know their self-worth as this helps them understand who they are. Socially, they are open to people when it comes to the shame they feel, which makes people admire and support individualists. This will often boost the confidence of a type four because they are quick to doubt themselves and their abilities (Cloete, n.d.).

Self-Preservation Category is Tenacity

Tenacity is the countertype for individualists and often makes people mistake them for a type one or type seven personality. Through self-preservation, type four personalities learn to live with their suffering, with some finding ways to overcome it. In fact, they often believe that it is their suffering which has made them stronger and able to manage various life circumstances. Because of this, they will often look for other people who they believe suffer in the same way they have so they can become a support system for them (Cloete, n.d.).

One-on-One Category is Competition

Type four personalities are not competitive when it comes to sports. Their competitive nature comes out when they have demands and want attention from other people in order to prove their self-worth. They become competitive when it comes to other people believing they are helpful, sensitive, compassionate, and generous individuals. Furthermore, individualists can become demanding when it comes to wanting people to listen to their emotions. In a sense, individualists want people to understand what they need and appreciate the struggles they face as sensitive people (Cloete, n.d.).

Relationships with Other Types

Depending on what level of integration individualists are in will influence how well they get along with other types. If they are at the healthiest level of integration, they can get along with nearly all the other personalities. However, when they are at a lower average and unhealthy level they will be less likely to have a healthy relationship with other personalities ("Relationships (Type Combinations)," n.d.).

Wing Types

One of the wings for type four personalities is type three. The advantages that the achievers bring to the individualists are helping them express their creative fantasies. Because of the type three personality, type four is able to balance their internal drama so that they can become more social. When they do reach their social setting, achievers will help them express their unique selves in a way that can engage other people. On top of this, type three will help the type four transform their life experiences in a positive way. The challenges that achievements bring to individualists are the feelings of having to hide their emotions and internalizing them as a way to control them. Achievers can also increase the feeling of sadness that type four personalities have because of the pressure individualists will feel towards achieving a certain level of success (Cloete, n.d.).

The second wing for individualists is type five. When it comes to the advantages that type five brings, it is teaching individualists to take things less personally. They also help them control their emotions and help them feel less detached from the world. On top of this, they can help them think logically and observe society objectively. The challenges that individualists face with type five are overdramatizing their self-image in a negative way, struggling to connect with other people, and becoming more withdrawn from society so they can hide their emotions easier (Cloete, n.d.).

Center Points

Individualists are part of the heart center. If you have a type four personality, you want to know why you are different from other people (Cloete, n.d.). You are proud of your individuality, which can be both a strength and weakness towards your character. Furthermore, type fours tend to internalize their shame, which is often how they begin to create their unique character.

Type four's strengths:

- Compassion

- Feeling deeply
- Empathy
- Creative
- Idealistic

Type four's weaknesses:

- Overly sensitive
- Dissatisfaction
- Demanding
- Self-absorbed
- Withdrawn
- Moody

How to Grow Personally

Keep Your Thoughts Positive

Keeping your thoughts positive will help you stay in the right mindset and avoid lengthy negative conversations with your imagination. Once you are able to accomplish this, you will begin to increase your self-esteem and confidence. Over time, you will find that you are able to turn negative life experiences into more positive experiences, which will help you grow and learn as an individualist.

One of the facts about being a type four personality, is you might never feel like you've found your true place in this world. You will often feel, whether you admit it to yourself or not, that you are unique and hold special characteristics unlike many other people. When you start to feel this way, you have to remember to maintain a positive mindset. You need to realize that the best thing you can do is remain unique but not allow yourself to become too withdrawn from society (Cloete, n.d.).

Use Self-Discipline to Help Manage Your Emotions

When you use self-discipline in your daily life, you will find that you start to feel less stressed and are able to manage your emotions better. It is important to know that self-discipline can show itself in many forms, from following a daily schedule to make sure you take time to meditate or any other way to release your negative emotions. For example, you will want to get enough sleep so that you will be better able to manage your emotions and struggles of being highly sensitive and individualistic. Furthermore, making sure that you find time for yourself so you can release any negativity will help you gain better control over transforming your negative thoughts into positive ones (Cloete, n.d.).

Don't Procrastinate

Another helpful way to grow your personality is to not procrastinate. Part of this you will learn through self-discipline. The other part you will learn as you stop procrastinating. Individualists will often put off tasks until they feel ready to do them. This happens because they feel like they have to prepare themselves in order to take on what they need to accomplish. However, there is never truly a correct time to do everything, especially if you are not looking forward to what you are doing.

Procrastination can make your emotions stronger, especially when it comes to negative emotions, such as stress. Therefore, once you stop procrastinating and start working on your tasks when you need to, you will find you are more capable of handling your emotions. Furthermore, you will start to gain self-confidence and believe that your self-image is more positive overall. Procrastination can interfere with a positive mindset, therefore, you want to do what you can to work on your tasks as soon as possible (Cloete, n.d.).

Chapter 6: The Investigator

The investigator's growth line runs from point five to point eight while its stress line runs from point five to point seven. The primary words used to describe the investigator, who is also referred to as the observer and the specialist, are innovative, isolated, perceptive, and secretive. Some popular investigator personalities are Siddhartha Gautama Buddha, Stephen Hawking, Vincent van Gogh, Tim Burton, and Kurt Cobain ("Type Five," n.d.).

What is the Investigator?

The biggest desire of a type five personality is to be knowledgeable and skillful. The biggest fear for an investigator is to be perceived as useless and incapable. Investigators are able to focus on very detailed and complicated tasks and tend to be insightful. They are also very curious and can become preoccupied by their thoughts and the situations around them. The biggest motivators for a type five personality are learning, being able to defend themselves from society with their knowledge, and being able to understand the environment and people around them ("Type Five," n.d.).

Investigators are the personality type who want to find out the truth. They not only want to learn the truth, but they want to know the in-depth version of the truth. They want to know every detail, why something happened, when it happened, and how it happened. Unfortunately, this can also cause investigators to think that they can never fully function in today's society. In fact, they can become more withdrawn because they are afraid of what is going to happen ("Type Five," n.d.).

Of course, this feeling is only escalated because type five personalities believe they can't accomplish tasks like other people can. They don't often possess the strong self-confidence that most other personalities do, which can often hold them back from becoming successful.

For investigators to fully understand why something is happening, they have to be able to observe it. They will then take the time they need to understand what they saw, heard, and why it happened. They are critical thinkers and will take the time they need in order to reach a conclusion. Of course, this can cause issues when it comes to deadlines and communicating with other people. This can often make people think that investigators procrastinate. However, they don't often procrastinate like most other personalities do. Instead, they are just taking their time so they can learn what happened and reach their own conclusion ("Type Five," n.d.).

Because of their observation and critical thinking skills, type five personalities are often creating and inventing new things. Because they want to see how things work, they are able to take something apart, put it back together, or create something new. These skills make investigators feel confident as they start to believe they can make their own place in this world. At the same time, their need to observe, learn, and create can often cause them to become more withdrawn from society. While they are fine with having a select group of friends, they do tend to feel lonely ("Type Five," n.d).

One of the biggest struggles for investigators is they don't like to face their problems head on. Because of this, they often have trouble forming relationships and in general struggle with functioning in society, especially within groups of people. In fact, one of the biggest obstacles investigators can face is having to accomplish a task in a team. They are much better at performing tasks individually ("Type Five," n.d.).

Levels of Integration

Healthy Levels

The healthiest level for an investigator is level one. Type five personalities who reach this level are open-minded. They also tend to be pioneer investigators. They will often spend their time figuring out new ways to accomplish tasks.

A level two can gain a lot of insight through everything they experience in their life. They have a strong ability to concentrate on tasks but can become too drawn into the task and can cause them to lose sight of what they needed to originally do. They are very observant, mentally alert, and good at predicting what will happen in the future because of their observational skills (Cloete, n.d.).

A level three will always look for something new to learn. They will often become an expert in their field of study, are highly independent, and skillful masters (Cloete, n.d.).

Average Levels

An investigator at a level four will often try to find new ways to do something. They will view things as a challenge, which will in turn help them to absorb the information they want to learn. They are often busy gathering as many resources as they can, so they can increase their knowledge. It is around this level where the investigator starts to become in-tune with their skills and works on ways to master their talents (Cloete, n.d.).

A level five will start to fall victim to their fantasy world. While they remain curious and continue to expand their knowledge, they also become detached from the things they learn and the ideas this knowledge puts into their head. It's during this phase that they start to focus more on dark topics, which can contribute to their increasingly morbid thoughts as they get trapped within their mind (Cloete, n.d.).

An investigator at level six is deemed argumentative and pessimistic. While they continue to learn, they don't focus on growing their knowledge like investigators do in the healthy level or the higher average levels. A type five personality would rather not have people interfere with their thoughts and tend to withdraw from society (Cloete, n.d.).

Unhealthy Levels

A level seven investigator is not only aggressive but highly unstable. They are victims of their dark thoughts, which often leads them to become repelled by other people. As a result, they become increasingly isolated from society (Cloete, n.d.).

An investigator who is at a level eight starts to become horrified by their increasingly dark thoughts. While they continue to dive into these thoughts, they become frightened by them and often realize that they are unhealthy. However, most do their best not to focus on how shockingly horrible their thoughts are as they become progressively obsessed with them (Cloete, n.d.).

The unhealthiest level for an investigator is a level nine. At this point, a type five personality will often suffer a psychotic break. They are often diagnosed with various mental disorders such as schizophrenia (Cloete, n.d.).

Subtypes of the Investigator

Social Category is Totem

One reason a type five personality is called the investigator is that they often carry characteristics that are associated with investigators. People who fit this personality type tend to look into the details of situations around them. They want to know why something happens and how it happened. They will often do their own research or talk to people in order to find out what is going on. They don't tend to listen to what other people say, partially because they are also known to disconnect themselves from other people. By disconnecting themselves, they are able to better manage their emotions and thoughts, which can help them have a clear mind when they are learning (Cloete, n.d.).

Self-Preservation Category is Castle

Investigators are believed to be introverts because they tend to withdraw from society. They keep close to a small number of friends, and they like to remain in their home as this helps keep their social boundaries clear. At the same time, they can often be seen observing people and situations as they try to figure out what is going on around them and why. Their need to be left alone in their home can often create a negative effect because they can find themselves protecting their privacy at an intense degree, which makes it hard for them to let their guard down if they need help from others or if people want to socialize with them (Cloete, n.d.).

One-on-One Category is Confident

Investigators will feel a lot of compassion and become very passionate towards a couple of people in their private life. However, this can help them to thrive socially, or it can cause them to test their partner or friends to make sure that they will not be harmed or betrayed by them. A type five personality might test their partner because they are afraid of letting their guard down. At the same time, investigators can become overly protective of their partner because they don't want to share this person with anyone else (Cloete, n.d.).

Relationships with Other Types

Like with the other personalities, investigators can get along with any type of personality. However, they are more compatible with type three personalities and less compatible with type two. Any personality that a type five gets to know can help them thrive or in other cases, cause more struggles. However, because a type five is typically non-confrontational, they won't often express how they feel. Instead, they will start to withdraw from people and society as a whole ("Relationships (Type Combinations)," n.d.).

Wing Types

One wing type for the investigator is a type four, also known as the individualist. Type four can help type five find a balance within their life, especially when it relates to how passionate they become about certain people. Other strengths include connecting with others, learning how to connect their emotions to their thoughts, and connecting themselves to their intuitions. The challenges that the investigator faces due to this wing type include becoming attached to fantasies, becoming depressed because they feel misunderstood by society, and withdrawing further away from society to avoid confrontation (Cloete, n.d.).

The second wing type for the investigator is a type six personality. The strengths that type six brings to type five include being able to understand someone else's point of view, increasing their connection with groups of people, and increasing their self-confidence so they become more comfortable in social settings. The challenges that a type five may experience from a type six are becoming more socially withdrawn because they believe they can't trust people and think that they will upset people if they continue to be overly social (Cloete, n.d.).

Center Points

If you have a type five personality, you are a part of the head center (Cloete, n.d.). You think that you have to know everything about the situation before walking into it. Therefore, you will often observe everything about what is going on, so that you know exactly what to expect.

Type five's strengths:

- Intellectual
- Dependable
- Self-reliant
- Calm
- Thoughtful

- Respectful

Type five's weaknesses:

- Overthinking
- Hoarding
- Isolation
- Detached

How to Grow Personally

Learn to Relax

Investigators often struggle with learning to relax. This can make them more intense, which can cause them to withdraw from people because they don't want to cause any problems, especially since they also don't like confrontation. Therefore, type five personalities need to take extra care to make sure they are able to unwind and find something, such as a hobby, that will help them relieve some of the stressors in their life. For example, going out for a walk, riding a bicycle, or joining a gym are great ways to relieve stress. However, some investigators are highly creative, which means that they might be able to relieve their stress through art or writing (Cloete, n.d.).

Avoid Distractions

Type five personalities are curious about everything, which can cause them to be easily distracted. When this happens, they often forget about the tasks they have to accomplish or else fall behind on them, which leads to the need of an extension on their deadlines or pushing the work aside. Therefore, it is important to make sure you accomplish your tasks, even if it means you need to use self-discipline or find techniques that will help you stop from getting too distracted by situations that aren't as important (Cloete, n.d.).

Don't Get Trapped by Your Thoughts

Because investigators are always thinking and trying to learn new things, they can easily become trapped in their own thoughts. When this happens, they tend to avoid the people around them and further withdraw from society. Because this can make an investigator feel lonely over time, often leading them to depression, it is important to make sure that they schedule social time into their calendar. Even if you only have a few friends, which many personalities are comfortable with, you will still want to make time to go to the movies, go out to eat, or hang out with them and play video games at home. This will help you keep a balance in your life so you don't feel trapped by your thoughts (Cloete, n.d.).

Chapter 7: The Loyalist

The stress line for the sixth personality type, the loyalist, heads to line three. The growth line goes from point six to point nine. The primary words used to describe a loyalist are responsible, suspicious, engaging, and anxious. Some famous people who exhibit a loyalist personality are Prince Harry, Mel Gibson. Mark Wahlberg, Julia Roberts, Mark Twain, Malcolm X, and Robert F. Kennedy ("Type Six," n.d).

What is the Loyalist?

Those with a type six personality are known to be excellent troubleshooters. Typically, they are able to problem-solve quickly and are considered to be hard-working, dependent, and trustworthy. Some of their motivations include support from other people, security, and being able to fight off their fears and anxiety. Because loyalists can often foresee the future, they become defensive and cautious of situations that can create undesirable results ("Type Six," n.d.).

The basic desire for a loyalist is to feel secure and have support from the people surrounding them. The biggest fear of a loyalist is losing the guidance and support they have from people closest to them. Out of all nine personality types in the

Enneagram theory, they are known to be the most loyal to their close friends and family. In fact, they can become just as loyal to their thoughts and beliefs as well. However, if they reach an unhealthy level, they can become withdrawn, aggressive, and exhibit signs of paranoia ("Type Six," n.d.).

One downside to a type six personality is they tend to lack self-confidence. This is why they often seek guidance and approval from other people. They think that they are not able to perform tasks which other people can. If they can't find someone that can guide them to reach a healthy balance, they will be their own guidance through the use of their imagination and what they believe is right ("Type Six," n.d.).

Loyalists are part of the thinking center, which means that they are constantly thinking. At the same time, they are easily afraid of their own thoughts. This often occurs because they have an internal fear that they are going to be wrong and cause problems for other people. This is why they are known to have high levels of anxiety.

It is often due to the anxiety a loyalist feels that will lead them to an unhealthy level of integration. Loyalists are often aware of their anxiety, therefore, they do what they can to try to combat their thoughts ("Type Six," n.d.). If they are successful, they are more likely to follow a healthy level of integration. However, if they are not successful, they will be more likely to fall victim to an unhealthy level of integration.

Because their anxiety is so strong, they will often spend time looking for the reasons that are causing their anxiety. Sometimes, they will realize there is no reason for their anxious behavior over something minor.

The biggest challenge that a type six personality faces is trying to build their safety net, so they can do their best to remain at a healthy level of integration ("Type Six," n.d.). They also want to build this form of security, so that they can protect themselves against their anxiety, thoughts, and emotions. They believe that if they are able to build a safety net, they will be able to deal with the stresses of life.

Levels of Integration

Healthy Level

Loyalists at the healthiest level, meaning level one, are some of the most positive thinkers. They have full trust in their feelings and beliefs, and are known to be independent. They have courage, are very trusting of other people, and believe in true equality (Cloete, n.d.).

At level two, a loyalist believes that trust is important and that most people can be trusted. They are known to have very strong relationships with others and feel deeply (Cloete, n.d.).

A loyalist who is at a level three is hard-working, trustworthy, responsible, and have a strong sense of community involvement. They often dedicate themselves to social movements which they strongly believe in. They believe that the world can become a secure place for everyone and are willing to sacrifice themselves in order to make this happen (Cloete, n.d.).

Average Level

A loyalist who is at a level four enjoy schedules, organization, and structure. They will spend the majority of their time trying to improve environmental conditions for other people, however, they won't always think their actions through. Their main focus is to make everything and everyone safe and secure (Cloete, n.d.).

A level five loyalist starts to become passive-aggressive when they think that people are taking advantage of them or asking them to take on too much. They experience an internal confusion on how to better themselves and their negative thought patterns, which can cause them to become angry and annoyed at other people (Cloete, n.d.).

A loyalist who is at a level six will often blame other people for their problems and become very insecure about the person they are. They are highly suspicious of other people because they believe that people cannot be trusted. They are known to be sarcastic, defensive, and argumentative. As a result, many loyalists tend to withdraw from society (Cloete, n.d.).

Unhealthy Level

A loyalist who is at a level seven will become very unstable and defenseless. They will look for an authoritative figure who can teach them how to defend themselves and, when they find one, they tend to become very dependent on this authoritative figure. However, they tend to struggle with relationships, which often drives them further into isolation. Loyalists at this level can become increasingly lonely (Cloete, n.d.).

Loyalists who are at a level eight tend to become paranoid. They think that people are out to get them and that no one can be trusted. They often turn to violence when they feel fear (Cloete, n.d.).

A loyalist who is at a level nine is often classified as someone with avoidant personality disorder or paranoid personality disorder. They often turn to thoughts of suicide because they want to escape their thoughts of paranoia and self-destructive behavior (Cloete, n.d.).

Subtypes of the Loyalist

Social Category is Duty

Type six personalities who are part of this subcategory are often compared to type one personalities. This is because they both share similar characteristics. Loyalists will do what they can to help those who they believe are weaker than them. They are also strict on making sure they follow rules and guidelines. They are known to be hard-workers and will do whatever they can to make sure they succeed in the tasks they are assigned (Cloete, n.d.).

Self-Preservation Category is Warmth

Loyalists are often afraid of making a mistake, which is why they don't share their ideas or opinions. They are known to be caring and warm individuals who tend to get along with any type of personality. In fact, they often spend their time with people because they enjoy the company of others. At the same time, they can have an internal fear about people noticing their insecurities (Cloete, n.d.).

One-on-One Category is Intimidation

This subtype is the countertype of the loyalist. They are often bold and typically aren't afraid to take the steps they need to take in order to defend themselves. They are known to be emotionally and mentally strong individuals that may run towards danger instead of away from it, no matter how much fear they feel. Loyalists under this subtype can be viewed as intimidating (Cloete, n.d.).

Relationships with Other Types

Type six personalities tend to become a strong friend or partner for any personality type. While they tend to become fast friends with personalities nine, two, three, and four, they can still face struggles with these types of personalities. Of course, a type six personality is also able to mix well with another type six personality. However, they will often find themselves trying to avoid confrontation because they share a lot of the same characteristics ("Relationships (Type Combinations)," n.d.).

Wing Types

One wing type for the loyalist is a type five personality. The strengths which the investigator brings to the loyalist are opening them up to being more accepting of other viewpoints, keeping their fears in check through analysis, allowing them to trust their internal validations, and feeling more confident in themselves. The challenges loyalists face with investigators include increasing their anxiety levels and avoiding confrontation (Cloete, n.d.).

Another wing type for the loyalist is a type seven personality. The strengths that this personality brings to the loyalist includes trusting other people, being optimistic, and feeling comfortable within society. The weaknesses that type seven brings to a type six personality are giving them ideas on how to escape situations so they can avoid confrontation and a fear of pain along with anxiety over trivial matters (Cloete, n.d.).

Center Points

If you have a type six personality, you are part of the head center and more likely to think of the worst possible outcome when faced with a danger (Cloete, n.d.). This is your natural reaction to danger because you believe it will help you prepare for what can possibly happen. While you generally look to authoritative figures for guidance, you will also rebel against them because you believe they become too attached and you want more independence from them.

Type six's strengths:

- Critical-thinking

- Strategizing
- Bravery
- Sensitivity
- Humor
- Loyalty

Type six's weaknesses:

- Overly energetic
- Anxiety
- Pessimism
- Hyper-vigilant

How to Grow Personally

Understand Anxiety is Normal

Many people in the world experience anxiety. In fact, anxiety is a part of all nine personality types in the Enneagram theory. Once a loyalist remembers that they are not different from the other personality types because of their anxiety, they are better able to deal with the stresses of life. Loyalists often think that they are the only ones who deal with anxiety, even though everyone experiences different types of anxiety. Some people experience anxiety over trivial situations and thoughts. Worry is part of everyone's daily life. On top of this, everyone is able to learn techniques to help them deal with their insecurities and anxious thoughts (Cloete, n.d.).

Learn What Your Stressors Are

Stress and anxiety go hand in hand. Therefore, when you are able to identify what your stressors are, you will be able to learn how to manage them accordingly. You learn to control your anxiety and your anxious thoughts (Cloete, n.d.).

Become More Trusting and Self-Confident

When a loyalist is at a healthy level, they are very trusting and self-confident. Every loyalist can reach this level and one way to do so is by learning to trust other people. Type six personalities need to learn that they can trust that others think they are generally good people. They need to believe themselves that people don't think of them in a negative way and that this is just a part of their anxiety and anxious thinking. If they are able to shift their mindset to this, they will become more trusting and self-confident (Cloete, n.d.).

Chapter 8: The Enthusiast

The stress line for the enthusiast runs from point seven to point two while the growth line runs from point seven to point five. The primary words used to describe a type eight personality are acquisitive, spontaneous, scattered, and versatile. Well-known people who are considered enthusiasts are Thomas Jefferson, Amelia Earhart, Robert Downey, Jr., Charlie Sheen, Paris Hilton, and Larry King ("Type Seven," n.d).

What is the Enthusiast?

Some of the main motivators for the enthusiast are freedom, keeping themselves occupied, happy, and avoiding pain. Their main fear is being in pain while their main desire is to know their needs are fulfilled. Type seven personalities are known to be very high-spirited, playful, have many talents, optimistic, and undisciplined. While they are always looking for something new to do as they enjoy seeking new and exciting adventures, they can also become easily exhausted from their adventures ("Type Seven," n.d.).

They are very curious about life and tend to look at the world with big and exciting eyes. In fact, many people would say they are similar to a kid in a candy shop. While they are very cheerful, they can also be domineering ("Type Seven," n.d.).

While they are at the head or thinking center, this doesn't necessarily mean that they think things through before making decisions. In fact, they can be very impulsive. At the same time, they are able to focus on their thoughts and are very practical. In fact, some people often say that enthusiasts have two personalities that can switch in an instant ("Type Seven," n.d.). For example, they can go from being very playful and impulsive to behaving in an adult-like way and think thoroughly before they act or speak.

Type seven personalities love to learn and will often spend their time looking for new information to take in. Therefore, they are known to be quick learners. Because of this, they are also able to pick up new skills ("Type Seven," n.d.). They tend to value their skills, which can also cause conflict as they struggle to determine what career path to take in their lives.

Enthusiasts are often out of touch with their thinking center, which is what causes them to sometimes become impulsive ("Type Seven," n.d.). This can also cause problems for people who are trying to guide them into a healthy direction of integration. In return, a type seven personality can experience feelings of anxiety. When they start to feel anxious, they will cope with it by becoming busy with something. At the same time, they can sometimes struggle with making the right choices.

Levels of Integration

Healthy Level

Enthusiasts at a level one are often in awe of the world around them. They are highly grateful for what they have in life and believe that people act with the best intentions. They believe that people want to work together to make the world a better place. They also believe that we are continuously succeeding in this effort (Cloete, n.d.).

A level two enthusiast is very spontaneous and is considered an extrovert. Like the first level, they believe that people share a common good and are very enthusiastic about where the world is going. They believe that we will make the world a better place, especially if we continue to work together (Cloete, n.d.).

An enthusiast who is at a level three tends to focus on certain areas of their community when trying to do the best for others. They are very realistic about their goals and are known to be high achievers (Cloete, n.d.).

Average Level

An enthusiast at a level four is more focused on money and trends than trying to make the world a better place. They aren't happy with the choices that life has given them and often look for better experiences (Cloete, n.d.).

A level five enthusiast has a fear of becoming bored with tasks and the people around them. Therefore, they are known to be very outgoing and loud. On top of this, they are known to be hyperactive. They make good performers. Furthermore, they often have trouble knowing what they need and what they want (Cloete, n.d.).

An enthusiast who is at a level six is very materialistic, greedy, and self-centered. This can make them very demanding as they often think they never have enough. For example, they more money they make, the more money they want to receive the next time. They are never truly grateful for what they have in life (Cloete, n.d.).

Unhealthy Level

An enthusiast who is at a level seven can become abusive and aggressive. They can often become addicted to drugs and alcohol and have trouble knowing when to stop, especially when they know they want something. They tend to have a lot of problems with money because they don't know how to manage their money (Cloete, n.d.).

An enthusiast who is at a level eight cannot control their impulses. At this point, their anxiety can reach a whole new high as they start to realize they can't control themselves. They also start to act out due to their impulses and frustrations when they can't get something they want (Cloete, n.d.).

A level nine enthusiast is often diagnosed with bipolar disorder as they go fluctuate between severe highs and severe lows. They have trouble coping because they realize they cannot manage their stresses and impulses. It is often at this stage that many enthusiasts start to contemplate suicide (Cloete, n.d.).

Subtypes of the Enthusiast

Social Category is Sacrifice

The sacrifice is the countertype for the enthusiast. This subtype will often sacrifice their needs in order to make the world a better place, especially for the people they love and support. At the same time, they want to become noticed for their sacrifices, thereby causing them to become judgmental of others if they are not recognized for their efforts (Cloete, n.d.).

Self-Preservation Category is Network

A type seven personality is typically considered extroverted as they enjoy hanging out with people, especially their close friends and family. They know how to help people and are often willing to do so, especially if it will bring more fun into their group. However, they might find themselves becoming too involved in pleasing others as this can become a motivator for them, which can send them into an unhealthy level of integration (Cloete, n.d.).

One-on-One Category is Fascination

Enthusiasts are known for their optimism and enthusiastic nature, which is how they received their name. However, they can become overly obsessed with the fantasy of making sure the world becomes a better place that they tend to forget about reality. When they see what the world is really like, they start to see the world as a gray place. This can often cause them to believe that the people they hang out with are boring and unwilling to help them turn the world into a more colorful and happier place (Cloete, n.d.).

Relationships with Other Types

While a type seven personality can get along with any other personality type, they mainly form relationships with types two, three, seven, and nine. In fact, they get along best with type nine personalities. Of course, as it is with any personality type, there are strengths and weaknesses brought on by these relationships ("Relationships (Type Combinations)," n.d.).

Wing Types

One of the wing types for a type seven personality is a type six, otherwise known as the loyalist. Like with any wing, the loyalist can bring about strengths and challenges into their relationship. The strengths that a type six can bring into the lives of a type seven includes commitment and a deeper understanding of their actions, mindfulness, and the act of taking things more seriously. The challenges that the loyalist brings to the enthusiast includes exaggeration of their fears, feeling like responsibilities are a burden, self-doubt, and the feeling of being irresponsible (Cloete, n.d.).

The second wing type for the enthusiast is a type eight personality. The strengths that the type eight brings with them includes assertiveness, learning how to plan better, becoming less afraid of feeling hurt, and learning to be honest with themselves and others. The challenges that type eight brings to an enthusiast are turning their assertiveness into aggression, wanting immediate satisfaction, and becoming self-absorbed (Cloete, n.d.).

Center Types

If you have a type seven personality, you are part of the head center and will try to turn your uncomfortable, fearful situations into something that is more exciting and comfortable (Cloete, n.d.). This occurs because people who are a type seven have a fear about becoming trapped in fearful situations. Therefore, they will do what they can in order to make themselves feel less fear.

Type seven's strengths:

- Energetic
- Quick-thinker
- Strong imagination
- Playful
- Optimistic

Type seven's weaknesses:

- Impatient

- Self-absorbed
- Unrealistic
- Isolation
- Uncommitted

How to Grow Personally

Control Your Impulses

Once you learn to control your impulses, you will be able to make better decisions and realize that you can't have everything exactly the way you want it and when you want it. Once you come to this realization, you will be able to judge whether you really need something, or you just want something. On top of this, you will get a better sense of what is good for you and what isn't (Cloete, n.d.).

Listen to People

When you start listening to other people, you will start to learn more than you ever thought possible. You will start to make better decisions because you will believe that others want the best for you and, therefore, won't send you down an unhealthy path. You will also learn that other people can be very interesting, and that they can help you become a better person. Furthermore, you will learn to enjoy your time alone because the more you connect with people, the more you will realize that you need your solitude to help you remain relaxed (Cloete, n.d.).

Chapter 9: The Protector

A type eight personality is called the protector, otherwise known as the controller. This is because while they also focus on protecting their environment, they also want to remain in control of everything and everyone around them. However, another name for the protector is the challenger. The stress line for the protector runs from point eight to point five and the growth line from point eight to point two. A few of the most common terms used to describe the type eight personality are decisive, confrontational, self-confident, and willful. Some of the most well-known people who follow in the path of the protector are John Wayne, Bette Davis, Roseanne Barr, Aretha Franklin, and Martin Luther King, Jr. ("Type Eight," n.d).

What is the Protector?

The protector is known to be strong, self-confident, protective, resourceful, and assertive. At the same time, they can also become domineering and feel the need to control everything around them. The main desire of a type is to be able to protect themselves. Their fear is being controlled by other people or being harmed by someone. The same way they want to protect their environment and others, they also want to be able to protect themselves ("Type Eight," n.d).

Some of the main motivations for type eight personalities are being able to resist their weaknesses, showing their strengths, being able to control their environment, and becoming self-reliant (Type Eight,"n.d).

One of the biggest reasons why the protector is often referred to as the challenger is because this type of personality is the one that is most likely to challenge themselves and other people ("Type Eight," n.d). In fact, they like to see how far they can go and in turn become self-confident when they see they are succeeding in tasks they deem challenging.

Type eight personalities are often referred to as protectors because they have to control their environment. While some people might see this as domineering, type eight personalities do this in order to protect everything around them, including themselves and other people. Protectors feel the need to have complete control of the environment so they can protect everyone, including themselves ("Type Eight," n.d).

A type eight's biggest fear is harm, however, there is another part to this fear. Not only does this include harm to themselves, but it also includes harm to other people and their environment. From a young age, protectors realize that they will have to be persistent and strong if they want to become the protectors they believe they need to be. This is because they know they will need to do their best to make sure no harm comes to themselves or others. Therefore, while their biggest fear is harm on others and the environment, they are more likely to fear loss of control than actual harm. This is because they realize they have to keep control in order so that they, others, and their environment may remain unharmed ("Type Eight," n.d).

Even though they are afraid of being harmed, they can usually take on a lot of physical harm. This is because they are known to be emotionally, mentally, and physically tough. However, they can handle physical harm a lot better than emotional and mental harm. In fact, they would rather be harmed physically. This is because they hold their health at a very high standard and often take it for granted ("Type Eight," n.d). Of course, this can cause issues with other personalities because type eight personalities are less likely to take care of their overall health and instead care for the well-being of other people.

Type eight personalities focus on protecting their environment. While the protector believes he or she is doing the right thing, people will think otherwise. This can throw the protector off-guard and wonder why people think otherwise when he or she works so hard to make sure that everyone is taken care of and protected. When this happens, they tend to become emotionally distant from the people closest to them. Unfortunately, when a type eight feels this way, he or she will also distance themselves from the rest of society ("Type Eight," n.d). This happens because the protector feels misunderstood and rejected, which in turn is a form of emotional harm.

Levels of Integration

Healthy Level

Protectors at a level one are their own masters. They are self-restrained, courageous, and willing to put themselves in physical harm in order to get what they want. Protectors at this level are often seen as heroes as they are constantly working towards protecting their environment and others over themselves (Cloete, n.d.).

Type eight personalities who are at a level two are known to be very strong and self-confident. They know what they want and what they need, and can become very assertive when it comes time to take action. They have an attitude of knowing that they can truly take over the world (Cloete, n.d.).

Protectors at a level three are natural-born leaders. People tend to look up to them as they are very authoritative and commanding. They do what they have to do to make sure that action takes place. In general, this level of type eight personalities are seen as very caring, strong, protective, great providers, and honorable (Cloete, n.d.).

Average Level

Protectors at a level four have a strong need for financial independence. They know what resources they need in order to gain this independence and are not afraid to become risk-takers or work hard in order to achieve it. While they can be seen as protective towards others, their main aim is to get what they want. They don't often ignore their own needs in order to help others; they ignore their own needs in order to reach the financial independence they want (Cloete, n.d.).

A level five type eight personality not only focuses on dominating their environment but also other people. Instead of seeing this as a form of protection, many people start to see this as a form of control. This is because they have a very boss-like demeanor and can become very forceful. At this level, protectors will start to believe that people aren't treating them with respect they deserve, therefore, they are not considered as equals (Cloete, n.d.).

Protectors who are at a level six are known to be extremely intimidating. In fact, at this level, people with other types of personalities start to become afraid of what they are capable of. They can become very confrontational and loud in order to get what they want. They do not like to back down and will continue to use threats in order to get other people to listen to them (Cloete, n.d.).

Unhealthy Level

Protectors who are at a level seven are at one of the highest unhealthiest levels. At this point, they become completely dictatorial in order to get people to listen to them and have control over them. While other personalities will start to band against them, they will become ruthless and make sure that they stay on top. Protectors at this level are known to be violent criminals and con-artists (Cloete, n.d.).

Protectors who are at a level eight often develop delusional thoughts about the power they hold. They believe they are untouchable (Cloete, n.d.).

Type eight personalities who are at a level nine are known to have sociopathic tendencies. They will destroy everything and anyone in their path if they feel threatened. In fact, they would rather destroy themselves than have to surrender to anyone else. Protectors at this level are barbaric and often show symptoms of antisocial personality disorder (Cloete, n.d.).

Subtypes of the Protector

Social Category is Solidarity

Solidarity is seen as the countertype for a type eight personality. Protectors in this group will often be viewed more as a type two than a type eight. This is because they tend to focus more on helping others, which makes them push aside their needs and wants. Protectors under this subtype have a strong sense to help the world socially by focusing on social issues that they think are important. They don't like to see injustice and they are very sensitive when it comes to the needs of other people. At the same time, they will become a shield for anyone they think is facing some form of injustice (Cloete, n.d.).

Self-Preservation Category is Satisfaction

Many people can view the protector of this subtype to have two distinct personalities. First, people will see this person to be very caring and generous. They typically take on a very comforting nature and can become a guardian or role model to many people as they take on the role of a mother, father, aunt, uncle, or sibling. In this role, type eight personalities will do whatever they can to help the people who need their help. However, they also believe that they should be able to get just as much in return. This is when people see a different side to this subtype as they can become aggressive and manipulative when they want something. While they will make sure everyone else's needs are satisfied, they will make sure their own needs are satisfied as well (Cloete, n.d.).

One-on-One Category is Possession

Type eight personalities who are a part of this subtype will be viewed as leaders and rebels. They will do whatever they need to do to make sure they reach the top and get to where they want to be. This subtype can easily be mistaken for a type four personality because they can become very impulsive when they want something. However, they do not have the characteristics of a type four personality. They are, in fact, acting this way because they become unapologetic when they want to reach a goal (Cloete, n.d.).

Relationships with Other Types

Like with the other personality types, type eight personalities tend to get along with other type eight's ("Relationships (Type Combinations)," n.d.). The relationship will progress if all the personality types are at a healthier level of integration, rather than an unhealthy level. However, this doesn't mean that the protector will not experience conflict when it comes to other personality types. For example, a relationship with a type three personality can also become too much of a good thing for the protector. Because they are both very positive when at a healthy level of integration, they will ignore the challenges they face together. This means they tend to avoid confronting each other when there are disagreements. Instead, they will keep their conflicts bottled inside and continue to work with each other. This can cause them to grow increasingly hostile towards each other.

Wing Center

One wing for the protector is a type seven. The strengths that this personality type brings to a type eight includes a balance with planning and perspective, happiness, the realization that they do not have to complete tasks alone, and knowing the value in expressing their thoughts and emotions. The challenges that a type eight may face are an increase in their addictive personality, the need to fulfill their desires, and become increasingly self-absorbed. They will also focus less on the consequences of their actions (Cloete, n.d.).

The second wing for a type eight is a type nine. This wing can bring many strengths and challenges to the protector. Some of the strengths are the realization that the protector does not need to make something happen if it can occur naturally, a sense of balance in life, and becoming more laid back and calm. The challenges include neglecting themselves, becoming out of touch with themselves, and withdrawing from society. When the protector begins to withdraw from those around them, they will feel guilty and will harshly judge themselves (Cloete, n.d).

Center Type

People who have a type eight personality are not only part of the body center but also tend to be known for their anger and temper issues (Cloete, n.d.). They externalize their anger, and are not afraid to show this emotion. However, they also want to protect themselves so they will often build guards as a means for protection. Most of the time, they will become angry because they think someone is being mistreated.

Type eight's strengths:

- Fairness
- Generosity
- Bravery
- Strength
- Honest
- Protective

Type eight's weaknesses:

- Forgetful
- Controlling
- Angry
- Lustful
- Afraid of showing vulnerability

How to Grow Personally

Use Your Power Wisely

One of the best ways to grow personally is to make sure that you use your power wisely. You have a strong sense of power and have the capability to do a lot of good with it, however, you have to know how to use it in order to not fall victim to an unhealthy level of integration. Unfortunately, when people hold a lot of power, it is natural for them to believe they want more of this power. However, if you act with self-restraint, you will understand that your power is used to help and uplift people instead of controlling them and the environment.

You are very helpful when it comes to dealing with a crisis. With your power, you are able to maintain a calm mind and make people feel more at ease when times are tough. This is a very special trait to have since you are the only personality which really holds this type of power. Therefore, it is important to make sure to use your power wisely and with good intentions (Cloete, n.d.).

Keep Your Ego in Check

Most personalities will struggle with their ego, regardless of if it's expressed externally or internally. As a protector, you often use your ego to protect yourself. Therefore, when your ego starts to build up, you will start to believe that you have to protect yourself more from other people and factors within the environment. When this happens, you will become more sensitive to any slight disrespect or to someone threatening your environment. This can cause you to act out, sometimes violently. In order to maintain a healthy level of integration, you will want to make sure your ego is kept in check so you don't start to overthink perceived threats (Cloete, n.d.).

Chapter 10: The Mediator

The type nine personality is called the mediator, or otherwise known as the peacemaker. This is because their primary descriptive words are agreeable, complacent, reassuring, and receptive. They are also known to be very easy-going, accepting, and trusting. Their stress line runs from point nine to point six and their growth line runs from point nine to point three. Some of the most well-known people who are known to be mediators are Queen Elizabeth II, John F. Kennedy, Jr., Abraham Lincoln, Janet Jackson, Jim Henson, and Walt Disney ("Type Nine," n.d).

What is the Mediator?

Some of the mediators' biggest motivators are bringing peace into their environment, being able to resist something that can disrupt them, and being able to avoid conflict. Their biggest desire is to have a peace of mind while their strongest fear is separation or loss. In a nutshell, they are known to be supportive, creative, and accepting. In fact, one of the biggest reasons they are often referred to as peacemakers over mediators is because they are the personality that will do everything in their power to bring peace into their environment and the lives of others ("Type Nine," n.d).

At the same time, type nine personalities will go above and beyond to ignore what is wrong in the world and with other people ("Type Nine," n.d). They don't like confrontation, therefore, they will use whatever means they can to bring peace into the situation and environment. If they are unable to bring peace into a situation, they will often react by becoming numb.

Mediators can also become out of touch with reality. When this happens, they often retreat to their mind and create a fantasy world, which allows them to continue to cope with what is going on around them, whether bad or good. This is when type nine personalities will start to use their personality powers against themselves ("Type Nine," n.d). They will feel so out of balance that they will start to struggle within their daily life.

However, when type nine personalities are able to remain balanced, they will be able to use their powers to help people in difficult situations. When they become in-tune with what they can do, they will use their energy to make peace with the situation. When they reach this level, they are able to critically think about the best way to solve the situation in a peaceful way rather than try to ignore the problem ("Type Nine," n.d). After all this, they will begin to think that if they cannot bring peace to the whole problem, then an issue still exists. Therefore, mediators think it is best to resolve the problem right away so that it doesn't come back a second time.

Mediators are also known to be one of the most spiritual personalities of the Enneagram theory. This is because they are known to be spiritual seekers, who not only want to form a strong internal connection with people but with their environment and the universe as a whole. In fact, while they are always working to keep peace among people, they are also working to create harmony within the world itself. Therefore, in order for them to truly believe they are fulfilling their work, they have to keep an open mind, focus on relaxation, let go of tension, stay away from mental, emotional, and physical pain, practice patience, and believe in unity over separation ("Type Nine," n.d).

Levels of Integration

Healthy Level

A mediator at a level one has a strong sense of fulfillment and is one with themselves. They are happiest with their lives, have great relationships with other people, and hold strong connections to their environment (Cloete, n.d.).

Type nine personalities which are at a level two are emotionally stable and calm. They are very trusting of other people, who also view mediators as very trustworthy. They are also known to be extremely patient, good-natured, and genuinely care about people and the environment. Many people believe they lead simple and innocent lives (Cloete, n.d.).

Mediators who are at a level three are extremely supportive and want the best for others. They are reassuring, optimistic, and tend to have a calming influence on other people. They are thought to be natural-born healers and are great at bringing people together for the common good. Furthermore, they are strong communicators and empathetic to others ("Type Nine," n.d.).

Average Level

Mediators who are at a level four often show more fear than mediators who are at a healthy level. They tend to be known as people pleasers because they will often go by what other people want, even if it's the opposite of what they want. This is because one of their biggest fears is conflict, which means they feel more comfortable going with the flow (Cloete, n.d.).

Type nine personalities at a level five start to walk away from the problems surrounding them. They don't want to disengage, but they would rather not deal with the conflict. They also believe that if they ignore the problem, it will go away on its own. They will start to tune people out, along with their environment, so that they don't have to focus on what they believe isn't right. As a result, they will start to create a fantasy world for themselves as they withdraw from society ("Type Nine," n.d.).

Mediators who are at a level six won't completely ignore problems but they will minimize them and try to bring a type of peace into their environment. Sometimes, they don't care at what price. They become stubborn and take on magical thinking to help them come up with solutions to their problems that will make people happy. However, other people see mediators at this level as uncaring, uninterested, and unresponsive (Cloete, n.d.).

Unhealthy Level

Mediators who are at a level seven think that they can't take on the problems they face. Therefore, they start to disconnect from their environment and society. Because of this, they neglect themselves and can become a danger to themselves or others ("Type Nine," n.d.).

Mediators who are at a level eight will do anything in their power to block out what they don't want to see or hear. At this point, they start to become numb about the world around them. In fact, they can become so disconnected that they begin to struggle with daily functioning (Cloete, n.d.).

Type nine personalities at a level nine will create different types of personalities to help them cope with the stress they experience in their lives. This is commonly referred to as multiple personality disorder. They become disoriented and are not able to function in their day to day life ("Type Nine," n.d.).

Subtypes of the Mediator

Social Category is Participation

The mediator is known to be a social butterfly. They are typically very popular in their group setting because of their personality. As participants, they do whatever they can to make sure the people around them are happy, even if this means ignoring their own beliefs, stresses, and problems. They do this because they fear becoming a burden. Therefore, they often think it's best to deal with their problems themselves, or allow their closest friends and family to help them. While they don't like to burden others, a mediator at a healthy level will realize that he or she can't always deal with his or her problems alone and will ask for help when necessary. Participation is considered to be the countertype for the mediator (Cloete, n.d.).

Self-Preservation Category is Appetite

This type of mediator understands that they need to take care of themselves in the same way that they take care of others. Type nine personalities typically fall under this subtype when they also have a lot of type eight personality in them. They want to make sure people around them are happy and protected, including themselves. They have found, what they consider to be a healthy balance between taking care of other people, their surroundings, and themselves. They can quickly become upset when people come into their reality and try to ruin the balance they have created, which is usually when they start to form negative relationships with other personalities (Cloete, n.d.).

One-on-One Category is Fusion

This subtype of type nine personalities struggle to take care of themselves like they do other people. In fact, they believe by helping others, they are helping themselves. In ways, this does work because the mediators feel a sense of pride and comfort in their actions when they are helping other people. This help feeds their demands to take care of themselves. However, this can only work for some of their personal needs. Unfortunately, type nine personalities in this subtype tend to ignore or push away their issues or feelings about certain things because they want to focus more of their attention on others (Cloete, n.d.).

Relationships with Other Types

The mediator can have a healthy relationship with any other of the personality types. The mediator doesn't like confrontation, so this type of personality will often find techniques to avoid it. However, when they are faced with confrontation, they will try to do it in a way where they won't cause any emotional or physical harm to the other person. However, the way they go about doing this also depends on the mediator's level of integration ("Relationships (Type Combinations)," n.d.).

Wing Center

One wing for the mediator is the type one personality. The strengths that type one brings to the mediator includes giving them structure and focus over their perspectives, motivation to do what he or she needs to do, and offering support as the mediator works towards their goals. While mediators can take the time to make sure their tasks are completed, the support and help from type one is an important factor to help them achieve these tasks (Cloete, n.d.).

Another wing type for the mediator is type eight. This type will give the mediator strengths by not only helping them become more active but also giving them a sense of power. Furthermore, the protector will provide the mediator with a sense of balance, which will allow the mediator to flourish into a unique individual instead of being someone who follows the crowd. A type eight personality will also help the mediator become more confident and bold, which will allow them to protect themselves when they are feeling attacked (Cloete, n.d.).

Center Point

If you have a type nine personality, you are part of the body center and you will turn your anger into peace (Cloete, n.d.). This is why you are considered the peacemaker. You might find yourself simply ignoring things that make you angry because you do your best to maintain harmony for yourself and those around you.

Type nine's strengths:

- Non-judgmental
- Caring
- Approachable
- Supportive

- Great moderator
- Adaptive
- Caring

Type nine's weaknesses:

- Indecisive
- Forgetful
- Stubborn
- Avoidant

How to Grow Personally

Notice Your Emotions

It is important for the mediator to notice their emotions whether they are in a difficult situation or not. The more you realize that it is okay to have these emotions, the less likely you will try to disconnect from yourself, other people, and your environment. On top of this, you will be able to reach and remain at a healthy level of integration for your personality. This means that you will be able to face situations by thinking of the best ways to overcome negativity in a peaceful way and be able to continue your daily tasks to the best of your ability (Cloete, n.d.).

There is No Way to Avoid Conflict and Negativity

You also need to make sure that you are aware of what is going on around you. While you don't want to focus on negativity, it is a part of life. It will be part of your emotions, your environment, and the people around you. There is no way to completely avoid conflict and negativity. These are factors that will help you maintain a healthy level of integration if you learn to face them like you can anything else. This will become easier once you realize you have the power to do so. You have the power to change a negative situation into a positive one because of your peaceful nature. If you're wanting to withdraw from society because you're struggling, it is important to make sure you force yourself to continue on your path. In order to grow and improve your special personality, it's important to face your struggles, whether externally or internally. Doing this will help you become more mentally and emotionally engaged, which will only help you strengthen your powers (Cloete, n.d.).

Become Aware of Your Body

Not only do you want to become aware of your emotions, but you also need to become aware of your body and how you control your emotions. For example, if you start to exercise, you will increase your awareness of your body and how your body reacts to certain exercises. You want to become mindful of yourself. This will not only help you remain calm during a crisis, but it will also allow you to think more clearly and help you focus more on yourself, others, and the environment. You'll be able to see a problem coming before other people do, which means you will be able to bring peace to the situation before it escalates (Cloete, n.d.).

Examine How You Can Contribute to Problems

No one is perfect, no matter how hard you try to keep the peace. It is important for mediators to realize that they can make mistakes. For example, if you find yourself having issues with your spouse, you will want to take a step back and examine why these issues are occurring. You not only what to look at what you think your spouse is doing wrong but also how you contribute to the problem. Of course, this is not going to be easy, especially for a mediator. However, it is essential if you want to truly solve the problem in your peaceful ways (Cloete, n.d.).

Chapter 11: Testing

The only way you can truly find out what type of personality you have is to take the Enneagram test. This test is easy to find online or you can take it through a professional. You can find the Enneagram test at Eclectic Energies Enneagram Tests, which offers the test for free. You can also take the test at the Enneagram Institute.

About the Test

The Enneagram test will give you a series of questions and then tell you what personality you mainly fit into based on your answers. These are not complicated questions and focus solely on your personality. For example, the test might ask you if you consider yourself to be an overall happy person and then ask you to rate how happy or unhappy you are.

While there are many versions of the test, with a varying amount of questions, you are typically given pretty accurate results. The results will provide you with a list that shows you how influenced you are by each personality. You will also receive your main personality type, your second type, and so on. Therefore, you will also learn which personality type you are least likely to have.

However, this test will not just tell you what type of personality you have; it will also give you a detailed look at other parts of your personality, which you have already learned about in several chapters of this book. For example, you will learn about whether you are at a healthy, average, or unhealthy level of integration. You will also learn about your two wing centers, your center point, and your subtypes. At the same time, you will be able to get a sense of which personalities you relate to the most and which ones you will have more trouble getting along with.

Summary of the 9 Types and Their Subtypes

Because I have already discussed the nine personalities and their subtypes in detail, I won't focus heavily on them in this section. However, I also realize that you have been given a lot of information in this book, which can be overwhelming. Therefore, I did want to take time to give you a brief summary of the last nine chapters you just read.

The first personality type is known is the perfectionist. This is because they like to have everything in order and make sure to do their best at every task. The perfectionist's three subtypes are worry, zeal, and non-adaptability.

The second personality type is the helper. Because of their need to help others, this will be their main focus in life. However, this can also be a fault of theirs as they tend to forget about their own needs. Their three subtypes are ambition, privilege, and seduction.

The third personality is the achiever. People with this type of personality focus on becoming highly successful. Their three subtypes are prestige, security, and charisma.

The fourth personality is the individualist. This personality type is known to be highly sensitive and strives to make sure they are their unique self, even if they end up hiding it from a crowd. Their subtypes are shame, tenacity, and competition.

The fifth personality type is the investigator. They are known to pay close attention to detail. They want to know as much as they can about a situation and their environment and will spend a lot of time trying to figure things out. Their three subtypes are totem, castle, and confidence.

The sixth personality is the loyalist. They are given this name because they are loyal to others. Their main subtypes are duty, warmth, and intimidation.

The seventh personality is the enthusiast. They are known to be very outgoing and see the best in everyone and everything. They are very enthusiastic and optimistic. Their three subtypes are sacrifice, network, and fascination.

The eighth personality type is the protector and was given this name for a reason. They are known to be strong, resourceful, and are very protective of their environment. Their three subtypes are possession, solidarity, and satisfaction.

The ninth, and final, personality type is the mediator/peacemaker. This personality type is non-confrontational and will do whatever they can in order to maintain the peace around them. The three subtypes of the mediator include participation, appetite, and fusion.

Difference Between the Myers Briggs and the Enneagram

There are a lot of different personality tests that you can take. However, the Enneagram and the Myers-Briggs are two of the most common ones (Drenth, n.d.). This section will take a look at the differences between the two tests.

Nature vs. Nurture

One of the biggest differences between the two tests is that the Myers-Briggs tests focuses on nature whereas the Enneagram focuses on nurture (Drenth, n.d.). The Enneagram focuses more on the events that occur during your childhood. For instance, your childhood experiences, the good and the bad, will affect your personality when you reach adulthood. In fact, detailed reports of the personalities will often outline whether the problems you have in adulthood are a result of your mother or father.

The Myers-Briggs test looks at your personality type based on the moment you were born with it. While factors in your life can influence your personality, this test claims there are parts of your personality that have been a part of you since birth (Drenth, n.d.).

Unhealthy and Healthy

One of the biggest things you may have noticed about the Enneagram is each of the nine personalities has levels of integration, which range from healthy to unhealthy. These levels, according to the Enneagram, will continue to develop in your personality throughout your various life experiences. The Myers-Briggs test also focuses on the unhealthy and healthy psychological levels. However, the Myers-Briggs test states that you can possess a dominant level and an inferior level. While both of these levels are conscious in your personality, you don't notice your inferior level as well as your dominant level (Drenth, n.d.).

Conclusion

By now, you should be able to explain the Enneagram theory to anyone. You not only know the basic personality points, but you also know what their healthy, average, and unhealthy levels are. On top of this, you can identify their wing points, how they form relationships with other personalities, their subtypes, and their center type. With all these pieces, you cannot only identify what personality type you have but also help other people take the test and explain their personality types.

There is a lot of other information out there about the Enneagram theory. This book was a comprehensive look at the theory, however, you can learn more about yourself and others through further research on the Internet or through other books. Like many of the personalities have shown, people enjoy learning as much as they can about a topic they are interested in.

From this book, you should not only be able to take the test yourself and identify which personality you have, but also which level of integration you are on and what types of relationships you're capable of forming. It is important to do what you can to become the best person you can be, especially when you understand your personality better.

Bibliography

1 - The Reformer. (2019). Retrieved from https://enneagramawakeningschool.com/2019/01/09/type-1/.

Berkers, E. Introduction to the Enneagram. Retrieved from https://www.eclecticenergies.com/enneagram/introduction.

Cloete, D. Wings, Arrow Lines, Integration and Self-Mastery. Retrieved from https://www.integrative9.com/enneagram/wings-lines-integration/.

Cloete, D. 27 Subtypes, Instincts of Claudio Naranjo. Retrieved from https://www.integrative9.com/enneagram/27-subtypes/.

Dodge, A. Personality Tools: Understanding the Enneagram (from a Myers-Briggs expert) — Personality Type and Personal Growth | Personality Hacker. Retrieved from https://personalityhacker.com/understanding-the-enneagram/.

Drenth, A. Enneagram vs. Myers-Briggs / MBTI: Key Differences. Retrieved from https://personalityjunkie.com/12/myers-briggs-mbti-vs-enneagram/.

Enneagram Types. Retrieved from
https://www.enneagramworldwide.com/tour-the-nine-types/.

Enneagram Centres. Retrieved from
http://www.fitzel.ca/enneagram/triads.html.

How The System Works. (2017). Retrieved from
https://www.enneagraminstitute.com/how-the-enneagram-system-works.

Hussey, R. (2017). How to Use the Enneagram of Personality
for Personal Growth. Retrieved from
http://www.artofwellbeing.com/2017/11/01/enneagramofpersonality/.

O'Hanrahan, P. Instinctual Subtypes. Retrieved from
https://theenneagramatwork.com/instinctual-subtypes.

Relationships (Type Combinations). (2017). Retrieved from
https://www.enneagraminstitute.com/the-enneagram-type-combinations.

Three Centres of Intelligence. Retrieved from
https://www.theenneagramsingapore.com/three-centres-of-intelligence/.

Type 1 Subtypes. Retrieved from
https://www.personalitycafe.com/type-1-forum-

reformer/6097-type-1-subtypes.html.

Type Eight. Retrieved from
https://www.enneagraminstitute.com/type-8.

Type Five. Retrieved from
https://www.enneagraminstitute.com/type-5.

Type Four. Retrieved from
https://www.enneagraminstitute.com/type-4.

Type Nine. Retrieved from
https://www.enneagraminstitute.com/type-9.

Type Seven. Retrieved from
https://www.enneagraminstitute.com/type-7.

Type Six. Retrieved from
https://www.enneagraminstitute.com/type-6.

Type Three. Retrieved from
https://www.enneagraminstitute.com/type-3.

Type One. Retrieved from
https://www.enneagraminstitute.com/type-1.

www.ingramcontent.com/pod-product-compliance
Lightning Source LLC
Chambersburg PA
CBHW060355290526
45791CB00002B/516